Robert Moynihan is the co-founder and editor of *Inside the Vatican* magazine, the world's most well-informed, comprehensive monthly news magazine on matters at the heart of the Roman Catholic Church. With a knowledge of five languages, Moynihan studied at Harvard before obtaining a PhD in medieval history from Yale University. He is the author of *Let God's Light Shine Forth: The Spiritual Vision of Pope Benedict XVI*, and a seasoned Vatican analyst whose website www.themoynihanletters.com enjoys an international following.

ROBERT MOYNIHAN

PRAY FOR ME

THE LIFE AND SPIRITUAL VISION OF

POPE
FRANCIS

RIDER

LONDON · SYDNEY · AUCKLAND · JOHANNESBURG

1 3 5 7 9 10 8 6 4 2

Published in 2013 by Rider, an imprint of Ebury Publishing
First published in 2013 by Image, an imprint of the Crown Publishing Group,
a division of Random House Inc., New York, USA

Ebury Publishing is a Random House Group company

The Random House Group Limited Reg. No. 954009

Addresses for companies within the Random House Group can be found at:
www.randomhouse.co.uk

A CIP catalogue record for this book is
available from the British Library

The Random House Group Limited supports the Forest Stewardship
Council® (FSC®), the leading international forest-certification organisation.
Our books carrying the FSC label are printed on FSC®-certified paper. FSC
is the only forest-certification scheme supported by the leading environmental
organisations, including Greenpeace. Our paper procurement policy
can be found at www.randomhouse.co.uk/environment

Printed and bound by CPI Group (UK) Ltd, Croydon CR0 4YY

ISBN 9781846044052

Copies are available at special rates for bulk orders. Contact the sales
development team on 020 7840 8487 for more information.

To buy books by your favourite authors and register for offers, visit:
www.randomhouse.co.uk

CONTENTS

PART TWO

The Life That Formed Pope Francis
135

PART THREE

In His Own Words
179

PREFACE

When Pope Francis stepped out on the balcony of St. Peter's Basilica for the first time on the cool evening of March 13, 2013, the people in the square below and those watching around the world asked themselves: Who is this man? What does he believe? What will he do as the leader of the Church?

This book hopes to provide starting points to answer some of those questions.

Written in the two weeks after the papal election, *Pray for Me* is partly my eyewitness account of those early days. During that time I was present in Rome for his initial meeting with journalists, his first Angelus, his first Wednesday audience, the March 19 Mass inaugurating his pontificate, the Palm Sunday Mass on March 24, the Easter Vigil Mass on March 30, and the Easter Sunday Mass on March 31, 2013. The first part of this book is a collection of "dispatches from the front," if you will. Here is a bit of history in the making, captured as it was happening, in order to root the story of Pope Francis in facts, rather than speculation about what he might do in the future.

This is followed by two other parts that introduce readers to the man, his life, and his spirit, based primarily on his own words and the words of those close to him. First, a brief biography provides a context for understanding this man's origins: from his childhood in Buenos Aires to his assuming the Chair of Peter at the age of seventy-six. This section also includes a look at the spiritual influences behind the actions taken by this dedicated priest. The last part is a collection of his words on various subjects, offering a glimpse of Pope Francis's thoughts on fundamental philosophical and theological issues. This is a window into his understanding of the ultimate questions of importance to the human soul: What is faith? What is hope? What is joy?

I approached this material as a journalist, but also as a believer. While I have tried to present a clear journalistic approach to the material, my main goal was to offer readers a tool that can be used in many ways as a devotional. Written in the spirit of *lectio divina*, or reading (in this instance, writing) in a prayerful manner, you will certainly find ample information on the whos, whats, and wheres of Pope Francis's life. But *Pray for Me* is really geared for those who would like to accompany Pope Francis on his journey of faith in the months and years ahead. You may certainly read this book cover to cover, but I encourage you to use it as a tool for contemplation, one in which you can turn to any page and open a space for prayer and meditation on Pope Francis's life—and yours as well.

And that is the central point of this book: It offers readers an opportunity to journey alongside this new pope, not only by walking with him in the first days of his papacy, but also by allowing readers to experience the soul of this man, his strength, passion, and tenderness.

Case in point: The morning of March 31, 2013, on Easter Sunday, Pope Francis—pope for just two and a half weeks—was riding through the vast crowd in St. Peter's Square when he came upon a young boy suffering from cerebral palsy.

I was standing just a few feet away and watched as Pope Francis reached out of his jeep, embraced the child, and kissed him on the cheek. There, in the midst of thousands, he held the boy, whose parents and friends had raised up with extended arms. This was not a "photo opportunity" but an act of love that left many who witnessed it in tears. The inner man performing an outer act of love was a prayer in the greatest sense of the word.

So this book is intended to help those who are responding to the first request made by this pope to all of us, a simple request, from his heart: "Pray for me." Pope Francis is aware of his own frailty, his own imperfection, his own humanity. He knows that he needs the prayers of others, as we all do. He knows that the prayers of others can support him spiritually to be and to do, as a successor of Peter, what he must be and must do. In calling for prayers for himself, Pope Francis asks us as a community to care for the poor, for those treated unjustly, for the imprisoned and the suffering, for those who have lost hope, and also for him, that he may carry out his task with courage and humility.

If this book, *Pray for Me*, will help to create such a community, it will have served its purpose.

Rome, April 2, 2013

Pray for Me

INTRODUCTION

....

The Spirit of Pope Francis

The world was astonished at the simplicity of the man. When he appeared on the balcony of St. Peter's Basilica in Rome at 8:24 P.M. on the evening of March 13, immediately after his election as the new pope, he was dressed all in white, only white, without the traditional red *mozzetta*, the elbow-length red cape, often trimmed in ermine, worn by the Roman pontiff over his white cassock. (We later learned that his assistant, the papal master of ceremonies, Monsignor Guido Marini, had placed the red cape on the new pope's shoulders, but that he had shaken his head and said, "No.")

He stood silently for a while, gazing out over the crowd of some two hundred thousand. He did not speak.

It was this silence that struck all of us, because all of us understood that no words, whether few or many, could fully express all that might need to be said, all the feelings, all the hopes, all the concerns, of that man, at that moment. There was a modesty in his silence, and a wisdom; a modesty in recognizing that whatever words he chose might not measure up to the significance of this moment, a wisdom to know that simply standing there, all in white, was already an expression of who he was, and what he intended to do.

His silence was eloquent, and his smile told us that he was with us, waiting with us, standing with us. His silence spoke to us.

In St. Peter's Square, onlookers had been gathering for an hour, as the news that white smoke had spilled out of the chimney of the Sistine Chapel at 7:06 P.M. had spread through the city.

Many had not expected the election to come so soon. There had been black smoke the previous day, the first day of the conclave, at 7:42 P.M., signaling an initial failed vote. And in the morning, at 11:40, the second *fumata nera* (black smoke) arrived, signaling two more inconclusive votes. When no smoke had come by 6:00 P.M., we understood that there had been a fourth failed vote, and many felt that there would be black smoke again, and no pope until the next day, or the next.

So when the white smoke billowed out, there was much surprise. The conclave had ended rather quickly. The cardinals had decided. Had they elected Angelo Scola of Milan, another Italian after two "foreign" popes? Odilo Scherer of São Paulo, Brazil? Marc Ouellet of Canada? Gianfranco Ravasi, the biblical scholar who had been the head of the famous Ambrosian Library in Milan? Had they made a radical departure from tradition and chosen a man from the Far East, like Luis Tagle of Manila or Malcolm Ranjith of Colombo? Had they perhaps even taken the revolutionary step of choosing an American, and if so, who was it? The jovial, bighearted Cardinal Timothy Dolan of New York? The more reserved Capuchin friar from Boston, Sean O'Malley, who had won the hearts of the Italian people in previous days with his Franciscan simplicity, and who was known as a Latino because of his knowledge of Spanish and his work with Latin American immigrants to the United States?

Restaurants emptied, and the people of Rome hurried to the square to see who the new pope was.

It was dark now, and cool, and there was a slight drizzle. Many had umbrellas. Some stood silent, some chatted, some prayed. And around the world, people came to their television sets or to their computer screens to watch for the first glimpse of the man who would follow Pope Benedict XVI "in the shoes of the fisherman"—as the successor of St. Peter.

Then, shadows appeared behind the curtains. The curtains parted, and Cardinal Jean-Louis Tauran, a Frenchman who is the proto-deacon of the College of Cardinals, the first of the order of deacons among the cardinals (there are three orders of cardinals—deacons, priests, and bishops), stepped out on the balcony. It was Tauran's task to announce the name of the new pope. Another priest stood next to him, holding a microphone that was linked to the large video screens set up around the square, so that all would be able to hear his words.

Tauran, a brilliant scholar as a young man, has had health problems in recent years, at times affecting his ability to speak clearly. But on this occasion, he summoned all his strength, and he spoke the following words, loud and clear:

"Annuntio vobis gaudium magnum," he began. (I announce to you a great joy—these words echo those of the angels to the shepherds in Bethlehem at the birth of Jesus, given in the

Gospel of Luke, 2:10: "Behold, I announce to you tidings of great joy.")

"Habemus Papam!" (We have a pope!) The crowd cheered. And then Tauran gave the new pope's name: *"Eminentissimum ac reverendissimum dominum, dominum* Giorgium Marium, *Sanctæ Romanæ Ecclesiæ Cardinalem* Bergoglio . . ." (The most eminent and most reverend lord, Lord *Jorge Mario,* of Holy Roman Church Cardinal *Bergoglio*).

Cardinal Jorge Bergoglio!

A Latin American pope! A pope from the New World, the first in history. And a Jesuit, the first Jesuit pope.

The Church had a Spanish-speaking pope, a pope who had become known for riding the bus rather than taking a chauffeured car. A pope "of the people."

And then Tauran gave us the name Bergoglio had chosen to be called:

"Qui sibi nomen imposuit . . ." (Who upon himself has imposed the name . . .)

"Franciscum."

Francis.

Francis? There had never before been a pope called Francis. Immediately, it seemed that he had been thinking of St. Francis of Assisi, the greatest of all the Western saints, the *poverello* (the little poor man) who had married "Lady Poverty."

Pope Francis. Pope of the poor, of the "little people," of the simple people. Of all of us. Several minutes later, Francis came out onto the balcony, dressed all in white, and stood silently.

PART ONE

A New Pope's
First Days

CHAPTER 1

....

The Head and the Heart

Pray for me.

—*Pope Francis, March 13, 2013, from the balcony of*
St. Peter's Basilica immediately after his election

The initial silence of the new pope struck all who saw him. And during those moments, as Pope Francis stood there smiling, seeming almost awkward, the world formed its first, and inevitably lasting, impression of the new bishop of Rome. It was a good impression. In his silence, Francis seemed to express a modesty, a humility, that the crowd below appreciated. Still, they desired to know him better, to understand who he was and what he intended to do.

But, for a moment, that desire was frustrated by the new pope's evident desire to remain "hidden" for just a little while longer, though the cameras of the world were trained upon him. And in that tension between words and silence, between a desire to know and a wish to remain hidden, a bond was formed between Francis and the people of St. Peter's Square.

How such things happen is not easy to explain. But before he said anything at all, the people had already begun to understand him, and to appreciate him. In his silence, in his modesty, in what appeared to be even a certain clumsiness, he was revealing, it seemed, his humanity, his sensitivity, and so spontaneous cries sprang up: *"Viva il Papa!"* "Long live the pope!"

A connection was formed. A type of communion. And we sensed that hidden from our sight were great depths of emotion, and great depths of thought, which were the source of a simplicity that drew us already into a relationship with him. Francis was not polished. He was not rehearsed. He was simply himself. A man dressed in white, standing in silence.

He had emerged as the leader of the Catholic Church at a very delicate moment. The previous pope, Benedict XVI, had stepped down from his post just two weeks before, flying in a helicopter from the Vatican to Castel Gandolfo, fifteen miles outside of Rome, in an unprecedented decision that had left many in the Church confused and uncertain.

One could not look at Francis standing there, smiling, seemingly at peace, without thinking: There is something in him, deep down, which motivates him, which energizes him, which informs his life. But we could not know at that moment what that "something" was. We were only to discover it slowly during the days that followed.

And so those first days of the new pope became in some ways like a detective story, where each action, each word of Francis, gave us a clue to who he is, and why. The mystery was: What is the source of this man's humility and strength? And the answer was: his faith.

We would discover later that he was drawing not upon the advice of clerical advisers, or media "spinmeisters," but upon deep wells of personal faith, wells whose sources were in the faith of his grandparents and parents and brothers and sisters, and his parish priest when he was a child, in the Marian piety of his youth, and in the books he had read, in the teachings of St. Augustine, St. Francis of Assisi, and St. Ignatius of Loyola, in the whole, rich culture of Argentine Catholicism in the 1930s and 1940s, leading to an unforgettable experience in 1953 of what he described as "God's mercy" toward him. It was then that he decided to commit his life to the cause of God in this fallen world.

In a talk on the Virgin Mary given on December 8, 2012, Pope Emeritus Benedict wrote something about Mary that seemed to describe also this initial moment of the new pope's silence: "I consider it important to focus on the final sentence of Luke's Annunciation narrative. 'And the angel departed from her.' The great hour of Mary's encounter with God's messenger—in which her whole life is changed—comes to an end, and she remains there alone, with a task that truly surpasses all human capacity." Benedict added: "May Mary Immaculate teach us to listen in silence to the voice of God, and receive his Grace which frees from sin and every selfishness so that we can taste true joy."

These words could serve as a preface to those first moments of encounter with the new pope. Here we were, rather unknowingly beginning a journey of exploration into the heart, mind, and soul of the man who had just taken that unusual papal name Francis.

DURING THE hour before the new pope appeared before the world and the citizens of Rome, he made a telephone call to Pope Emeritus Benedict XVI, to tell him he would visit him soon. Then, when all was ready, the cardinal proto-deacon Jean-Louis Tauran came to the balcony and at 8:12 P.M., one hour and six minutes after the white smoke, announced the name of the new pope.

The College of Cardinals had chosen Cardinal Jorge Mario Bergoglio, S.J., age seventy-six, archbishop of Buenos Aires, Argentina, to become the 266th pope of the Roman Catholic Church. Francis was only two years younger than Benedict XVI had been when he was elected, in 2005, but he was eighteen years older than Pope John Paul II, the predecessor of Benedict, who was fifty-eight when he was elected, in 1978.

The new pope's choice of a name was the first clue we had to his character, even before the new pontiff spoke a word. By choosing Francis instead of other possible names (Pius XIII, John XXIV, Paul VII, John Paul III, Benedict XVII, or even Leo XIV), the new pope was signaling that he would chart his own course, break new ground— and that he would do so in great simplicity, and out of deep love for the poor of this world.

At 8:22 P.M.—ten minutes after the announcement by Cardinal Tauran—Pope Francis, preceded by the cross, appeared on the loggia of the basilica, to greet the people and to impart his first apostolic blessing, *Urbi et Orbi* (to the city of Rome and to the world). Beside him on the balcony stood Cardinal Cláudio Hummes, O.F.M., of Brazil. This was unusual, against normal protocol. Normally only the pope's vicar for Rome (Cardinal Vallini), and the Vatican secretary of state (Cardinal Bertone), along with the papal master of ceremonies (Monsignor Marini), would be expected to stand with the new pope on the balcony. Later we would learn that Pope Francis had insisted that Hummes stand with him at that moment. This, too, seemed a clue to the man and his program, for Hummes has criticized the spread of global capitalism, claiming it has contributed to "misery and poverty affecting millions around the world." And Pope Francis would later reveal that he had been inspired to take his name from St. Francis of Assisi by Hummes, his good friend, who had whispered to him after his election but before his choice of a name, "Don't forget the poor." At the very least, it showed how Francis could privilege a personal friendship at a moment of great solemnity.

> Brothers and sisters, good evening.
> You know that the duty of the conclave was to give a bishop to Rome. It seems that my brother cardinals went almost to the end of the world to get him. But here we are.
> I thank you for your welcome. The diocesan community of Rome has its bishop. Thank you!
> First of all, I would like to say a prayer for our Bishop Emeritus Benedict XVI. Let us all pray together for him, that the Lord will bless him and that our Lady will protect him.

The crowd then joined him as he prayed for Benedict, in Italian, the Our Father, the Hail Mary, and the Glory Be to the Father.

"And now let us begin this journey," Francis said.

> Bishop and people. This journey of the Church of Rome which presides in charity over all the Churches. A journey of brotherhood, of love, of trust between us.
> Let us always pray for one another. Let us pray

for the whole world, that there might be a great sense
of brotherhood.

My hope is that this journey of the Church
that we begin today, together with the help of my
Cardinal Vicar, here present, may be fruitful for the
evangelization of this beautiful city.

And now I would like to give the blessing. But
first, first, I want to ask you a favor. Before the
Bishop blesses the people I ask that you would pray
to the Lord that he bless me—the prayer of the
people, asking a Benediction for their Bishop. Let us
say in silence this prayer, of you over me.

So once again, there was silence. The silence of prayer.
Prayer not of the pope for the people, but of the people for
the pope. Then Francis spoke again.

"I will now give my blessing to you and to the whole
world, to all men and women of good will."

And he gave his blessing, in Latin, in the name of the
Father, and of the Son, and of the Holy Spirit.

Brothers and sisters, I am leaving you. Thank you
for your welcome. Pray for me and I will be with you
again soon. . . . We will see one another soon.

Tomorrow I want to go to pray to the Madonna,
that she may protect all of Rome. Good night and
sleep well!

In these first words of his pontificate, Francis did three
noteworthy things: First, he spoke of Pope Emeritus Benedict as "Bishop [of Rome] Emeritus Benedict." He did not
use the words "Pope Emeritus" to refer to Benedict. Second,

he asked the people to pray that the Lord bless him as he began his pontificate, before giving his own blessing of the people. Third, he said he would go the next day to "the Madonna," at the Basilica of St. Mary Major, where there is an icon of Mary and the child Jesus, traditionally believed to have been painted by St. Luke, called the *Salus Populi Romani*, the Protection of the Roman People.

And so, in his first words, Francis set the tone of all that was to follow, one of humility, one of prayer.

Clearly, here was a pope with a deep Franciscan and Marian spirituality. Yet if his strength came from his faith, where had his spirituality come from? What did it mean to him? What could it mean to us? And why had he begun with a request for prayer for himself? Why had he humbly asked: "Pray for me"?

Who Is Francis?

The press was soon flooded with reports about the life of this surprising new pope, this choice predicted by almost no one, especially the oddsmakers. Within hours news began to emerge that put the election of Bergoglio in a new light. Apparently, as had been rumored but never confirmed, the Argentine cardinal had been a strong candidate for the papacy in 2005, though he himself had supported Joseph Ratzinger. In fact, as many as forty cardinals, many wishing to block the election of Benedict XVI, had evidently voted for Bergoglio, even against his will, until, at lunch in the Domus Santa Marta on April 19, 2005, the final day of the conclave, it is said, Bergoglio made a negative sign with his hand, indicating that he preferred the cardinals not vote for him any longer.

These reports made clear that, far from being a surprise, Bergoglio should have been considered the leading candidate in 2013. Despite his age of seventy-six, the cardinals thought the archbishop of Buenos Aires should be the next pontiff.

THE SIGNIFICANCE of his choosing the name Francis cannot be overstated. It is a reflection of his life. Having become archbishop of Buenos Aires in 1998, he had left the comfortable episcopal residence next to the cathedral and gone to live in an apartment a short distance away, together with another elderly bishop. In the evening, Bergoglio did the cooking. He took the bus to get around the city. And he kept his distance from the Roman Curia, even after Pope John Paul II made Bergoglio a cardinal, in February 2001. "On that occasion, Bergoglio distinguished himself by his reserve among his many more festive colleagues," Italian Vaticanist Sandro Magister noted in 2002. "Hundreds of Argentinians had begun fund-raising efforts to fly to Rome to pay homage to the new man with the red hat. But Bergoglio stopped them. He ordered them to remain in Argentina and distribute the money they had raised to the poor. In Rome, he celebrated his new honor nearly alone—and with Lenten austerity."

In short, Bergoglio is a man whose words are matched by his actions. A man who does what he asks others to do.

"There isn't a politician [in Argentina], from the right to the extreme left, who isn't dying for the blessing of Bergoglio," Magister wrote. "Even the women of Plaza de Mayo, ultraradicals and unbridled anti-Catholics, treat him with respect. He has even made inroads with one of them in private meetings. On another occasion, he visited the deathbed of an ex-bishop, Jeronimo Podestá, who had married in defiance of the Church and was dying poor and forgotten by all. From that moment, Mrs. Podestá became one of his devoted fans."

He is a man who is able to seek out the poor, the ostracized, the abandoned.

And note well: "Someone in the Vatican had the idea to call him to direct an important dicastery," Magister wrote. " 'Please, I would die in the Curia,' Bergoglio implored. They spared him."

He is not a man who desired to be in the Roman Curia, or would have chosen to become its head.

The Vatican's Official Biography

The Vatican quickly released an official biography that contained the key facts of Bergoglio's life and some colorful particulars.

The first Pope of the Americas, Jorge Mario Bergoglio, hails from Argentina.

The seventy-six-year-old Jesuit Archbishop of Buenos Aires is a prominent figure throughout the continent, yet remains a simple pastor who is deeply loved by his diocese, throughout which he has traveled extensively on the underground and by bus during the fifteen years of his episcopal ministry. "My people are poor and I am one of them," he has said more than once, explaining his decision to live in an apartment and cook his own supper.

He has always advised his priests to show mercy and apostolic courage and to keep their doors open to everyone. The worst thing that could happen to the Church, he has said on various occasions, "is what de Lubac called spiritual worldliness," which means, "being self-centered."

And when he speaks of social justice, he calls people first of all to pick up the Catechism, to rediscover the Ten Commandments and the Beatitudes. His project is simple: if you follow Christ, you understand that "trampling upon a person's dignity is a serious sin."

Despite his reserved character—his official biography consists of only a few lines, at least until his appointment as Archbishop of Buenos Aires—he became a reference point because of the strong stances he took during the dramatic financial crisis that overwhelmed the country in 2001.

He was born in Buenos Aires on December 17, 1936, the son of Italian immigrants.

His father Mario was an accountant employed by the railways and his mother, Regina Sivori, was a committed wife dedicated to raising their five children.

He graduated as a chemical technician and then chose the path of the priesthood, entering the Diocesan Seminary of Villa Devoto.

On March 11, 1958, he entered the novitiate of the Society of Jesus. He completed his studies of the humanities in Chile and returned to Argentina in 1963 to graduate with a degree in philosophy from the Colegio de San José in San Miguel. From 1964 to 1965 he taught literature and psychology at Immaculate Conception College in Santa Fé and in 1966 he taught the same subject at the Colegio del Salvatore in Buenos Aires. From 1967 to 1970 he studied theology and obtained a degree from the Colegio of San José.

On December 13, 1969, he was ordained a priest by Archbishop Ramón José Castellano.

He continued his training between 1970 and 1971 at the University of Alcalá de Henares, Spain, and on April 22, 1973, made his final profession with the Jesuits. Back in Argentina, he was novice master at Villa Barilari, San Miguel; professor at the Faculty of Theology of San Miguel; consultor to the Province of the Society of Jesus, and also Rector of the Colegio Máximo of the Faculty of Philosophy and Theology.

On July 31, 1973, he was appointed Provincial of the Jesuits in Argentina, an office he held for six years. He then resumed his work in the university sector and from 1980 to 1986 served once again as Rector of the Colegio de San José, as well as parish priest, again in San Miguel. In March 1986 he went to Germany to finish his doctoral thesis; his superiors then sent him to the Colegio del Salvador in Buenos Aires and next to the Jesuit Church in the city of Córdoba as spiritual director and confessor.

It was Cardinal Antonio Quarracino, Archbishop of Buenos Aires, who wanted him as a close collaborator. So, on May 20, 1992, Pope John Paul II appointed him titular Bishop of Auca and Auxiliary of Buenos Aires. On May 27 he received episcopal ordination from the Cardinal in the cathedral. He chose as his episcopal motto, *miserando atque eligendo*, and on his coat of arms inserted the IHS, the symbol of the Society of Jesus.

He gave his first interview as a bishop to a parish newsletter, *Estrellita de Belém*. He was immediately appointed Episcopal Vicar of the Flores district and on

December 21, 1993, was also entrusted with the office of Vicar General of the Archdiocese.

Thus it came as no surprise when, on June 3, 1997, he was raised to the dignity of Coadjutor Archbishop of Buenos Aires. Not even nine months had passed when, upon the death of Cardinal Quarracino, he succeeded him on February 28, 1998, as Archbishop, Primate of Argentina, and Ordinary for Eastern-rite faithful in Argentina who have no Ordinary of their own rite.

Three years later at the Consistory of February 21, 2001, John Paul II created him Cardinal, assigning him the title of San Roberto Bellarmino. He asked the faithful not to come to Rome to celebrate his creation as Cardinal but rather to donate to the poor what they would have spent on the journey.

As Grand Chancellor of the Catholic University of Argentina, he is the author of the books *Meditaciones para religiosos* [Meditations for the religious] (1982), *Reflexiones sobre la vida apostólica* [Reflections on the apostolic life] (1992), and *Reflexiones de esperanza* [Reflections on hope] (1992).

In October 2001, he was appointed General Relator to the Tenth Ordinary General Assembly of the Synod of Bishops on the Episcopal Ministry. This task was entrusted to him at the last minute to replace Cardinal Edward Michael Egan, Archbishop of New York, who was obliged to stay in his homeland because of the terrorist attacks on September 11.

At the Synod he placed particular emphasis on "the prophetic mission of the bishop," his being a "prophet of justice," his duty to "preach ceaselessly" the social doctrine of the Church and also "to express an authentic judgment in matters of faith and morals."

All the while, Cardinal Bergoglio was becoming ever more popular in Latin America. Despite this, he never relaxed his sober approach or his strict lifestyle, which some have defined as almost "ascetic." In this spirit of poverty, he declined to be appointed as President of the Argentine Bishops' Conference in 2002, but three years later he was elected and then, in 2008, reconfirmed for a further three-year mandate. Meanwhile in April 2005 he took part in the Conclave in which Pope Benedict XVI was elected.

As Archbishop of Buenos Aires—a diocese with more than 3 million inhabitants—he conceived of a missionary project based on communion and evangelization. He had four main goals: open and brotherly communities, an informed laity playing a lead role, evangelization efforts addressed to every inhabitant of the city, and assistance to the poor and the sick. He aimed to reevangelize Buenos Aires, "taking into account those who live there, its structure, and its history." He asked priests and lay people to work together. In September 2009 he launched the solidarity campaign for the bicentenary of the Independence of the country. Two hundred charitable agencies are to be set up by 2016. And on a continental scale, he expected much from the impact of the message of the Aparecida Conference in 2007, to the point of describing it as the "*Evangelii Nuntiandi* of Latin America."

Until the beginning of the recent *sede vacante*, he was a member of the Congregation for Divine Worship and the Discipline of the Sacraments, the Congregation for the Clergy, the Congregation for Institutes of Consecrated Life and Societies of Apostolic Life, the Pontifical Council for the Family, and the Pontifical Commission for Latin America.

Phone Calls

But this official biography only begins to give us insight into the man himself. To understand Pope Francis, one has to look more closely at how he treats people. Especially ordinary people. How? Well, for one thing, with respect, by calling them on the phone and talking to them directly.

One of the first people he called on the day after his election was his younger sister in Argentina. She told Italy's daily Catholic newspaper, *Avvenire*, that she spoke to her brother on March 14.

Pope Francis called his sister to say he was okay, but he had another message as well. He said he wouldn't be calling the rest of the family so that the Vatican wouldn't get a high phone bill.

And then he called the father general of the Jesuit order, his former superior.

When he put the call through to the Curia of the Jesuits, just a couple hundred yards from the Vatican, the young doorman who answered thought it might be a joke, Catholic News Agency reported. Pope Francis had to patiently convince the doorman that he really was the pope and wished to thank the father general for a letter he had received upon his election.

According to Father Claudio Barriga, S.J., who recounted the incident in an e-mail to fellow Jesuits around the world, the unexpected phone call from the pope came around 10:15 A.M. Rome time.

The doorman answered the phone. They said it was a call from St. Martha's Residence and he heard a soft and serene voice: *"Buon giorno, sono il Papa Francesco, vorrei parlare con il Padre Generale"* (Good morning, it's Pope Francis. I'd like to speak with the Father General).

The doorman almost answered: "Yeah, and I'm Napoleon," but he resisted. Instead he replied curtly, "May I ask who's calling?" The Pope realized the young Italian man didn't believe it was him, so he kindly repeated, "Seriously, it's Pope Francis. What's your name?"

Ever since the Pope's election, our phone has been ringing every two minutes and a lot of people are calling, including a few lunatics.

Once the doorman realized his mistake he answered with a hesitant and nervous voice:

"My name is Andrew."

"How are you, Andrew?" asked the Pope.

"Fine, pardon me, just a little bit confused."

The Holy Father responded, "Don't worry, could you please connect me with the Father General? I would like to thank him for the beautiful letter he sent me."

"Pardon me, Your Holiness, I'll connect you right now," said the doorman.

"No problem. I'll wait as long as necessary," said Pope Francis.

The doorman handed the phone to the Father General's private secretary, Brother Alfonso.

"Hello?" Brother Alfonso said.

"With whom am I speaking?" the Pope asked.

"It's Alfonso, the Father General's personal secretary," he replied.

"It's the Pope, I would like to speak with the Father General to thank him for the beautiful letter he sent me," the Holy Father said.

"Sure, just a moment," Brother Alfonso replied in amazement.

As he made his way to the office of Father Adolfo Nicolás, the Jesuit Father General, he continued his conversation.

"Holy Father, congratulations on your election! We are all happy here for your election, we are praying a lot for you," Brother Alfonso told him.

"Praying that I keep going or that I turn back?" the Pope joked.

"That you keep going, of course," he replied, as the Holy Father laughed.

Stunned and bewildered, Brother Alfonso didn't even bother to knock and simply entered the office of the Father General, who looked at him with surprise. He gave him the phone, looked at him and said: "The Pope."

We don't know the details about what happened next, but the Pope cordially thanked the Father General for his letter. The Father General said he would like to see him to greet him. The Pope said he would instruct his secretary so that they could meet as soon as possible and that somebody from the Vatican would be in touch.

And the calls kept coming.

"He called the Archdiocese of Buenos Aires to check in before celebrating Mass in St. Peter's Square," said Father Javier Soteras, director of Radio Maria Argentina. "When a nun answered the phone, she asked, 'Who is calling?' and he said, 'Father Jorge.' The nun said, 'Your Holiness?' He said, 'Oh, c'mon, it's Father Jorge,' kind of referencing that it was not a time for official titles."

Pope Francis even called his Argentine dentist to cancel his appointments. Father Soteras explained, "It's his way of showing respect. It's obvious that he wouldn't be stopping by, but he wants to personally let these people know."

Pope Francis also showed tact and generosity by phoning his predecessor, Pope Emeritus Benedict XVI, on March 19, the Feast of St. Joseph (Benedict's original name was Joseph Ratzinger, so St. Joseph is his patron saint and the Feast of St. Joseph is also his feast).

The phone conversation was "long and cordial," the Vatican press office reported. Pope Francis renewed his expression of thanks to his predecessor for his long service to the Church, and Benedict XVI assured his successor of his prayerful support. Benedict had followed the inaugural Mass of Pope Francis carefully by television from Castel Gandolfo.

EVEN THOUGH Pope Francis is very close to his family, he would often skip their barbecues back home to spend Sundays or holidays in Buenos Aires's slums, his sister said. "That's the way he is: totally devoted to the mission of a priest; he is the pastor of the least," said Maria Elena Bergoglio.

The youngest of five, Maria Elena, sixty-five, is the pope's only surviving sibling, said a report in *Avvenire*, on March 19. She told the newspaper that she and her brother are extremely close, which she attributes to their parents' emphasis on the "the value of love."

"We've always had a very close relationship despite the twelve-year age difference. I was the youngest and Jorge always pampered and protected me," she said. "Every time I had a problem, I'd go running to him, and he was always there." Even though his ministry and duties kept her brother busy, the siblings spoke by phone every week, she said.

"Jorge taught me to always be there for people, to always be welcoming, even if it meant sacrificing something," Maria Elena said.

She said she named her firstborn son Jorge, "in honor of my special brother." He also became the child's godfather. The pope's nephew, Jorge, thirty-seven, told the paper that his uncle "is someone who is very open, we talk about everything, long talks."

Maria Elena said the media has been reporting on her brother's love of tango, opera, and soccer, but that very few people know he is an excellent cook. "He makes fantastic stuffed calamari; it's his favorite dish," she said.

She said she and her family stayed home in Ituzaingo, near Buenos Aires, to watch the pope's inaugural Mass on television out of respect for his public request that Argentines give to the poor the money they would have spent on airfare to be at the Mass in Rome. "We are near him in prayer," she said.

When her brother called her after his election, she "wasn't able to say a thing," because she was so overwhelmed with emotion, she said. "He just kept repeating, 'Don't worry, I'm fine, pray for me.'"

Just hours after Francis's dramatic election, an Italian journalist in Rome said one of the first things he did was call her up for a friendly chat. "The phone rang. . . . My son picked it up and it was the pope," Stefania Falasca, a former editor for the Catholic monthly *30 Giorni*, told Italian media.

"At home we just called him 'father,' we never called him 'eminence,' " she said. "I didn't know what to say. I asked him, 'Father, what am I meant to call you? Holy Father?'

"He laughed and he told me: 'The first phone call I wanted to make was to say hello to you, Gianni, and the kids,' " she said. Falasca is married to Gianni Valente, who was also a journalist with *30 Giorni* and now works with the Vatican's Agenzia Fides, a news agency and part of the Congregation for the Evangelization of Peoples.

A few days later, Pope Francis surprised the owner of a kiosk in Buenos Aires with a call to explain that he would no longer need a morning paper delivered each day.

Around 1:30 P.M. local time on March 18, Daniel Del Regno, the kiosk owner's son, answered the phone and heard a voice say, "Hi, Daniel, it's Cardinal Jorge." He thought that maybe a friend who knew that the former archbishop of Buenos Aires bought the newspaper from them every day was pulling a prank on him.

"Seriously, it's Jorge Bergoglio, I'm calling you from Rome," the pope insisted.

"I was in shock, I broke down in tears and didn't know what to say," Del Regno told the Argentine daily *La Nacion*. "He thanked me for delivering the paper all this time and sent best wishes to my family."

Del Regno said that when Cardinal Bergoglio left for the conclave, he'd asked the cardinal if he thought he would be elected pope. "He answered me, 'That is too hot to touch. See you in twenty days, keep delivering the paper.' And the rest is, well, history," Del Regno said.

"I told him to take care and that I would miss him. I asked him if there would ever be the chance to see him here again. He said that for the time being that would be very difficult, but that he would always be with us."

Before hanging up the phone, he added, the pope asked him for his prayers.

On March 19, the thousands of people who were spending a sleepless night in the main square of Buenos Aires, Plaza de Mayo, to watch the Mass inaugurating former archbishop Jorge Mario Bergoglio's Petrine ministry had a pleasant surprise. At 7:32 A.M. Rome time—that is, 3:32 A.M. in Argentina—the speakers placed outside the cathedral began to carry the voice of Pope Francis. He was calling from the Vatican to greet them.

As reported by the Argentine newspaper *Clarin*, the pope had called the cell phone of Father Alejandro Russo, rector of the cathedral. From the archdiocesan television center, they were able to connect the call to the Plaza de Mayo. Shortly afterward, those gathered began to hear Francis's voice. "Dear sons and daughters, I know you have gathered in the square. I know that you are saying prayers, I need them very much. We all walk united," he said. "We take care of each other, and continue to pray for me."

Once again, he was asking for prayers for himself. And then he explained why.

"To pray," he continued, "is so beautiful. It means looking to heaven and to our heart. We know that we have a good Father who is God."

Looking to heaven and to our heart. This brief definition of the meaning of prayer sums up the mind of the new pope, which moves from the most sublime things—heaven, the eternal, the absolute, the true, the good, the beautiful—to the most simple, down-to-earth things—the things in the human heart. The first is the realm that transcends all that we do, the realm that is not yet here but that we long for, hope for. The second is the realm of our most intimate privacy, the core of our being, the source of our identity, and of our hopes. And for Pope Francis, prayer connects these two realms. The furthest out, and the furthest in. And to pray, to bring about this "communion" between what is furthest out and furthest in, is radiant, he tells us.

It is an aesthetic judgment. To pray, he is telling us, before it is good, or true, or effective, or powerful, is "beautiful." And he says this because he knows the human heart, the human soul, is made to be drawn toward the beautiful, as a sunflower turns toward the sun, following it from dawn until dusk.

A huge roar of applause greeted the pope's words, and he continued: "I want to ask a favor of you. I want to ask for us to walk together, to care for one another, for you to care for each other. Do not cause harm. Protect life. Protect the family; protect nature; protect the young; protect the elderly. Let there not be hatred or fighting. Put aside envy."

And, in the city's slang, he added: *"No le saquen el cuero a nadie"* (literally, "Don't flay or skin anyone alive," that is, don't gossip, don't criticize one another). Talk with one another so that this desire to protect each other might grow in your hearts. And draw near to God. God is good. He always forgives and understands. Do not be afraid of him. Draw near to him and may the Virgin bless you. May she, as a mother, protect you. Please do not forget this bishop who is far away but who loves you very much. Pray for me!

"Through the intercession of Mary, ever Virgin, and each of your guardian angels, the glorious patriarch St. Joseph,

St. Therese of the Child Jesus, and each of your protector saints, may God Almighty, Father, Son, and Holy Spirit, bless you," Francis concluded.

We had in these words already the essentials of the program he would outline in a sermon in his early days as pope: protect the family, don't break it apart; protect our natural world, don't poison it; protect children, don't expose them to violence, don't harm them; protect the elderly, don't abandon them, respect them.

THE RESIDENTS of the area of Buenos Aires where Bergoglio was born and grew up, called *porteños*, describe Pope Francis as kind, outspoken, and a good administrator.

Oscar Justo, sixty, regularly begs for bills and coins on a perch next to St. Joseph Parish in Barrio de Flores. As Cardinal Jorge Mario Bergoglio, Pope Francis passed by often, walking from the bus stop or surfacing from a nearby subway station. But he always took time to greet Justo, offer a blessing, and provide a few pesos. "He always gave me something . . . sometimes a hundred pesos [twenty dollars]," said Justo, who lost both legs in a railway accident.

Such stories of his kindness abound in Buenos Aires, where Pope Francis was archbishop for fifteen years. *Porteños* came to know Pope Francis as an unpretentious prelate.

Cardinal Bergoglio criticized the late president Néstor Kirchner and President Cristina Fernández de Kirchner, who succeeded her husband in 2007, and their way of doing politics—building patronage groups instead of alleviating poverty, he alleged. They responded by going to other churches for important ceremonies. "They went off to the provinces . . . where there was a more friendly church," said José María Poirier, director of the Catholic magazine

El Criterio, who has interviewed Pope Francis frequently over the years.

"Here in Buenos Aires, he was a man politically at odds with the government, very much loved by the poor and members of the opposition. . . . But, fundamentally, he's a pastor and political man," Poirier said. "Bergoglio is very demanding. . . . He demanded a lot of discipline and obedience. He also considered himself a privileged interpreter of St. Ignatius of Loyola, and this caused controversy," said Poirier. "Half [of the Jesuits] liked him a lot, but half wanted nothing to do with him."

Gabriel Castelli, a member of the board of directors at the Pontifical Catholic University of Argentina, said the new pope "always had the ability to say what he thinks."

He put a priority on providing attention to his priests. He had a cell phone reserved just for his nearly four thousand diocesan priests, and each morning he set aside one hour to take their calls. "He was very committed to his priests, which is difficult with such a large archdiocese," Castelli said.

Priests had to keep their parishes in order, Poirier said. Many in the Church, like Poirier, speak of the former cardinal's administrative skills in Buenos Aires. "He's not an intellectual [like Pope Benedict], rather a man of government, with great political and administrative abilities," Poirier said.

Poirier said Pope Francis preferred the shanties to high society; he never dined out or went to parties; he read voraciously. He especially liked Latin American literature and Dostoyevsky novels. He did not use a computer or e-mail and listened to games of his favorite soccer team, San Lorenzo, on the radio.

He returned often to Barrio de Flores, to St. Joseph

Parish, where he was scheduled to celebrate Mass on Palm Sunday. At St. Joseph, parishioners shared memories.

"He always carried his own bags," recalled Zaira Sanchez, seventy-two. After Mass, "people would wait outside and he would bless all of them and talk to them" before leaving on public transit, she said.

He took time for causes, too—such as Fundación Al-ameda, which sought support from Cardinal Bergoglio for its efforts against the exploitation of migrants working in Argentina. The foundation's director, Olga Cruz, knew the then cardinal previously—he baptized both her children, who were not infants, after she asked him personally. "He said it would be an honor," recalled Cruz, a native of Bolivia.

Pope Francis embraced the migrants' cause, making public statements and celebrating Mass for the foundation. "He told me, 'Don't be afraid' . . . that I can confront this," Cruz told Catholic News Service. She also recalled him coming at a moment's notice to provide spiritual and moral support for women rescued from the sex trade, who were sometimes sheltered in parishes.

Parishioners at St. Joseph showed mixed emotions about Pope Francis having to leave Argentina for a higher calling. "Once he got to know you, he knew you for life," said Gloria Koen, seventy-three. "Unfortunately, we had to share him with the world."

CHAPTER 2

....

First Visit

Look into my heart, you know it better than me.
—*Pope Francis, prayer to the Blessed Virgin, April 19, 1998,*
Buenos Aires

On the first day after his election, Pope Francis did something remarkable and unprecedented. At about 8:00 A.M., he slipped out of the Vatican in a single unmarked black car—a Volkswagen, not a Mercedes—and, with a driver, rode across Rome to the Basilica of St. Mary Major, the largest and most beautiful basilica in the world dedicated to Mary, the Mother of God.

He walked into the church with just a few minutes of warning, strode across the length of the basilica, then stopped at the chapel in the far corner toward the back. There he placed a bouquet of flowers on an altar beneath an ancient icon of the Virgin Mary.

It was an act of chivalry, and act of love. It was the act of a son toward his mother.

And in this act, we could see clearly more of the inner life of this new pope. This pope was not about rules and regulations, although clearly, from all reports, he had been able to demand order from the priests of his diocese, and from his brother Jesuits. But close to his heart were gestures of love. Close to his heart was the thought, on the morning of the first full day of his pontificate, of visiting the spiritual mother he loved, and of bringing to her a bouquet of flowers. Who could not be touched by this act?

The image that Francis knelt in front of is called the *Salus Populi Romani,* or the Protectress of the Roman People. It is held to have been painted by St. Luke, the author of the Gospel that shows more than any other the suffering side of Christ's life and also of Mary's life. From at least the fifteenth century, this image was credited with healings. And it was later used by the Jesuits in particular to foster devotion to the Mother of God through the Sodality of Our Lady movement.

The *Salus Populi Romani* is only one of many so-called Luke images. But the tradition that this particular image is the original, and was painted by St. Luke himself when Mary was still alive, is very strong.

This is what legend tells us: After the Crucifixion, when Our Lady moved to the home of St. John, she took with her a few personal belongings, among which was a table built by Jesus himself in the workshop of St. Joseph. When pious virgins of Jerusalem prevailed upon St. Luke to paint a portrait of the Mother of God, it was the top of this table that was used to memorialize her image. While applying his paints, St. Luke listened as the Mother of Jesus spoke of the life of her son, which the Evangelist later recorded in his Gospel.

Whatever the factual truth of the pious tradition, this

icon is the single most important image of Mary that the Roman Catholic Church possesses. In venerating this icon, and through the icon Mary herself, Francis was following in the footsteps of many previous popes.

In A.D. 593, Pope St. Gregory had the icon carried through Rome and prayed for an end to the Black Plague. Pope St. Pius V in 1571 did the same, praying for victory at the Battle of Lepanto. Pope Gregory XVI in 1837 did the same, praying for the end of a cholera epidemic.

Pope Pius XII, when he was still Father Eugenio Pacelli, celebrated his first Holy Mass in front of this icon on April 1, 1899, and in 1953—the year Pope Francis committed himself to become a priest—the icon was carried through Rome to initiate the first Marian year in Church history. In 1954 the icon was crowned by Pope Pius XII as he introduced a new Marian feast Queenship of Mary. Pope Paul VI, Pope John Paul II, Pope Benedict XVI, and Pope Francis all honored the *Salus Populi Romani* with personal visits and liturgical celebrations.

But no pope has ever come so quickly to visit the icon. No pope has ever seemed so completely focused on doing honor and reverence to Mary before doing anything else. And that is why this first act of Francis's pontificate was so revelatory. By rushing across Rome just after dawn on the first morning after his election to bring flowers to the Virgin Mary, present in the form of the oldest and most precious Marian icon in the world, he was declaring his love for Jesus' mother.

So what is it about Mary that prompts such devotion?

For Catholics, and especially for preconciliar Catholics, Mary is central because she focuses all her life and attention on Jesus, leads all toward Jesus; because she was his mother, his protector, his defender; because she was the woman whose faith enabled her to be the "vessel" through whom Jesus was able to enter into the world; the woman who summed up in her own being all that was hoped for by the people of Israel throughout the ages; the woman whose purity, courage, and fidelity enabled those hopes to come to fruition in him whom Christians believe is the promised savior, the Messiah.

For Catholics, there is one great hymn that summarizes the spirituality of Mary and is central to the spirituality of Pope Francis. It is called the *Magnificat* (the Latin word means "[My soul] magnifies [the Lord]"). It is the song Mary herself composed when she visited her cousin, Elizabeth, the mother of John the Baptist.

The text of the song is recorded only in Luke (1:46–55). The other Gospels do not mention it.

> *My soul doth magnify the Lord : and my spirit hath rejoiced in*
> *God my Savior.*
> *For he hath regarded : the lowliness of his handmaiden.*
> *For behold, from henceforth : all generations shall call me blessed.*
> *For he that is mighty hath magnified me : and holy is his Name.*
> *And his mercy is on them that fear him : throughout all*
> *generations.*
> *He hath shewed strength with his arm : he hath scattered the proud*
> *in the imagination of their hearts.*
> *He hath put down the mighty from their seat : and hath exalted the*
> *humble and meek.*
> *He hath filled the hungry with good things : and the rich he hath*
> *sent empty away.*
> *He remembering his mercy hath holpen his servant Israel : as he*
> *promised to our forefathers, Abraham and his seed for ever.*

The meaning is clear: that God stands with the lowly, with the poor, with the humble, with the meek. And Pope Francis is a Marian pope. He is inspired by the spirituality of the *Magnificat.* This is fundamental to his mind and heart.

Pope St. Pius V and the Rosary

While in the Basilica of St. Mary Major, Pope Francis also bowed his head in prayer in front of the tomb of Pope St. Pius V (1504–1572), who promulgated the 1570 edition of the Roman Missal, making it mandatory virtually throughout the Latin rite of the Catholic Church. This form of the Mass remained essentially unchanged until Pope Paul VI's revision of the Roman Missal in 1969–70. It is what many today call "the old Latin Mass," or "the Tridentine Mass," or, since 2007, the "Extraordinary Form" of the Mass. It seems clear that by kneeling and praying before the tomb of this great and holy pope, Pope Francis was making a statement of respect for him and his work, and so, by implication, for the form of the Mass that he codified.

Also, while a cardinal, Pope Pius V gained a reputation for putting orthodoxy before personalities, prosecuting eight French bishops for heresy. And he stood firm against nepotism, rebuking his predecessor, Pope Pius IV, to his face when he wanted to make a thirteen-year-old member of his family a cardinal. For a pope like Francis, who wishes to end corruption, a prayer before the tomb of Pius V makes perfect sense.

Finally, Pius V arranged for the formation of the Holy League, an alliance of Catholic states that defeated the Ottoman Empire at the Battle of Lepanto in 1571. Pius V attributed this victory to the intercession of the Blessed Virgin

Mary and instituted the Feast of Our Lady of Victory on October 7. In 1573, Pope Gregory XIII changed the name of this feast day to Feast of the Holy Rosary. And this, too, was a hint about the spirituality of Pope Francis, because, as he has told us himself, he prays the Rosary daily.

In a tribute to Pope John Paul II written after the Polish pontiff's death, in 2005, and published in *30 Giorni* magazine, Cardinal Bergoglio recounted how the pope's example inspired him to "recite the fifteen mysteries of the Rosary every day."

"If I remember well, it was 1985," Bergoglio wrote. "One evening I went to recite the Holy Rosary that was being led by the Holy Father. He was in front of everybody, on his knees. The group was numerous; I saw the Holy Father from the back and, little by little, I got lost in prayer. I was not alone: I was praying in the middle of the people of God to which I and all those there belonged, led by our Pastor.

"In the middle of the prayer I became distracted, looking at the figure of the Pope: his piety, his devotion was a witness," he continued. "And the time drifted away, and I began to imagine the young priest, the seminarian, the poet, the worker, the child from Wadowice . . . in the same position in which he knelt at that moment, reciting *Ave Maria* after *Ave Maria.* His witness struck me."

Bergoglio added: "I felt that this man, chosen to lead the Church, was following a path up to his Mother in the sky, a path set out on from his childhood. And I became aware of the density of the words of the Mother of Guadalupe to Saint Juan Diego: 'Don't be afraid, am I not perhaps your mother?' I understood the presence of Mary in the life of the Pope.

"That testimony did not get forgotten in an instant.

From that time on I recite the fifteen mysteries of the Rosary every day."

So when Pope Francis prayed in front of the tomb of Pope Pius, what was emerging was an image of a man with a quite traditional Catholic piety, linked to an extraordinary humility and love of simplicity and the poor. But was there even more significance in this gesture?

After Pius V was elected, he proceeded to reduce the cost of the papal court. Early indicators suggest that Pope Francis will certainly look to cut the cost of the Vatican Curia.

As previously mentioned, we saw a sign of this simplicity and frugality when he instructed his nuncio in Argentina to ask all the bishops, priests, nuns, and faithful of his home country not to travel to Rome for his March 19 installation Mass, but to save the money and give it instead to the poor. "I have the honor and the satisfaction of turning to you to inform you that the Holy Father Francis has asked me to transmit to all Bishops, Priests, Religious men and women, and to all the People of God his cherished recognition for the prayers and the expressions of warmth, affection, and charity that he has received," Archbishop Emil Paul Tscherrig, the apostolic nuncio to Argentina, wrote. "At the same time, he would wish that, instead of going to Rome for the beginning of his Pontificate next March 19, you may keep this spiritual closeness that is so much appreciated, accompanying it with some gesture of charity towards the neediest."

The Pilgrim Virgin of Fatima

As archbishop of Buenos Aires, Pope Francis received the statue of the Pilgrim Virgin of Fatima on April 19, 1998. After the reception, the image of the Virgin went in procession to the College of Our Lady of Fatima, where the Eucharist was celebrated. Bergoglio gave a brief homily in which he reflected on the figure of Mary as the mother who welcomes and comforts all her children, knowing their prayers, wishes, and joys.

"Welcome home, Mother! Look for my family, you know what you need," he prayed. "Look through our neighborhood, you know right where to go. Look into my heart, you know it better than me. Welcome home!"

That was a prayer the pope can now repeat, but his neighborhood is no longer just Buenos Aires. It has become the whole world.

ON THE way back to the Vatican from St. Mary Major, the new pope asked his driver to circle back to the Domus Internationalis Paulus VI, a Vatican-owned guesthouse for visiting priests, bishops, and cardinals, where he had been staying in the days prior to the conclave.

He had left his luggage there. That was part of his reason for returning. But then he decided to stop at the front desk, say hello to the staff, and pay his bill. (It's not clear how much he paid, but "complete pension" rates at the Paulus VI are 85 euros, or about $110 per night.)

It was all in keeping with the new pontiff's reputation for frugality, the Vatican said.

Francis had been pope for only half a day.

CHAPTER 3

....

First Mass and Homily to
His Fellow Cardinals

> When one does not profess Jesus Christ—I recall the
> phrase of Léon Bloy—"Whoever does not pray to
> God, prays to the devil."
>
> —*Pope Francis to his cardinals in his first homily as pope*

At five o'clock in the evening of March 14, Francis celebrated his first Mass as pope. It was a Mass *Pro Ecclesia*
(for the Church), attended by the same cardinals who had
elected him in the Sistine Chapel the day before. The ceremony was televised live in Italy.

Several things struck observers about this Mass. First,
that Pope Francis went away from his throne and to the pul-
pit to speak his homily, like a classical preacher. Second, that
he wore very simple vestments. Third, that he spoke without
a prepared text. Francis could have asked someone to prepare
a text for him, and then he could have made small or large

revisions, but he preferred to deliver a spontaneous meditation, more direct, more familiar, more authentic.

He spoke for about seven minutes in beautiful Italian, slowly, clearly, eloquently. He structured his homily around three words: *camminare*, to walk; *edificare*, to build; and *confessare*, to confess or bear witness to the glory of Christ and his cross. He asked the cardinals to walk with him, and if they fell, to get up and start walking again; to build with him, to build the Church; and to confess Christ with him, but always, Christ with his cross.

"In these three readings," Pope Francis began, "I see a common element: that of movement." By using this word *movement*, Francis was already signaling something: that he wanted activity, life, action, work—movement—not a static, self-satisfied, immobile Church. And there was even a hint of his affection for the new "movements" in the Church, one of which, called Communion and Liberation, founded by the Italian priest Don Luigi Giussani (1922–2005) in 1954, he had come to appreciate greatly.

He continued: "In the first reading, it is the movement of a journey; in the second reading, the movement of building the Church; in the third, in the Gospel, the movement involved in professing the faith. To walk, to build up, to confess."

In these words, he was revealing his own program.

And then he cited the first verse of scripture of his pontificate, a line from the prophet Isaiah: "O house of Jacob, come, let us walk in the light of the Lord" (Is 2:5).

And he underlined the connection between this line in Isaiah and the very beginning of the journey of Israel, the journey that would lead to the promised land, and then to the birth of Jesus. "This is the first thing that God said to Abraham: Walk in my presence and live blamelessly," Pope Francis told his fellow cardinals. "To walk: our life is a journey, and when we stop moving, things go wrong. To walk always in the presence of the Lord, in the light of the Lord, seeking to live with the blamelessness that God asked of Abraham in his promise."

It was a call to moral living, to Christian living—to holy living. It was a call that resonated in the light of all the scandals that have plagued the Church in recent years, from the sins of priests to the infighting in the Roman Curia that had erupted in the "Vatileaks" scandal in 2012.

Then, speaking very simply, Pope Francis began to speak directly of his goal: "To build."

Immediately, many of those listening could sense that Pope Francis was echoing the words spoken to St. Francis of Assisi by Christ in a mystical moment as St. Francis prayed before the crucifix in the church of San Damiano in Assisi in the early 1200s: "Go, build up my church, which is falling down"—the words that sparked his vocation.

Pope Francis said to his cardinals: "To build up the Church. We speak of stones: stones are solid; but living stones, stones anointed by the Holy Spirit. To build up the Church, the Bride of Christ, on the cornerstone that is the Lord himself. This is another movement of our lives: to build up."

Clearly, Pope Francis was calling on his cardinals to join him in an effort to renew the Church by building spiritually on the "cornerstone," Christ, to create a living church of living stones, not simply a structure of beautiful marble and sculptures and windows.

And then Francis turned to his third word, "confess." He spoke slowly, almost as if in a private conversation: "Thirdly, to confess. We can walk as much as we want, we can build many things, but if we do not confess Jesus Christ, things go wrong. We may become a charitable NGO, but not the Church, the Bride of the Lord."

This was a key passage. When he said that the Church could become "a charitable NGO" (an NGO is a non-governmental organization, a philanthropic organization that carries out social activities), he was saying that the Church could lose her identity. He was laying down a marker once again, saying that the Church could not simply be a social welfare organization, but had to be something more, "the Bride of the Lord."

Then Pope Francis asked: "When we are not building on the stones, what happens?" And he answered his own question: "The same thing that happens to children on the beach when they build sandcastles: everything is swept away, there is no solidity."

This was a startling image. He was saying that the Church herself could be washed away, as a castle of sand is washed away on the beach, if she is not based on Christ, if she seeks any other basis, even the basis of good works. Only when based on Christ can she stand secure. Otherwise, she crumbles away under the pressures of the world. He was calling on the cardinals and all who listened to make a new commitment of the Church, in the Church, to Christ, as the starting point for any activity, for any movement, for any building.

And then he accentuated this thinking with a quite politically incorrect remark: "When we do not confess Jesus Christ, the saying of Léon Bloy comes to mind: 'Anyone who does not pray to the Lord prays to the devil.' When we do not confess Jesus Christ, we confess the worldliness of the devil, a demonic worldliness."

The reference to the devil came like a splash of cold water, unexpected. He had been speaking about Christ, and suddenly, he had shifted gears. He was saying that Christ was the Church's cornerstone, and suddenly, he was saying that abandoning Christ, turning away from Christ, leaving Christ aside to do "good things" without Christ, was not simply "missing" Christ; that is, was not simply "neutral," but was actually negating Christ, was embracing the devil, the evil one. These were dramatic words that came directly from the new pope's heart.

And then Pope Francis began to speak of the cross. His words had begun with walking, with building, and had seemed filled with a sense of rolling up sleeves and getting to work to accomplish great things, all in the light of day, under the sun. But now he spoke of shadows. Of problems. Of suffering.

"In journeying, building, confessing, there can sometimes be jolts," he said, "movements that are not properly part of the journey: movements that pull us back. . . . The same Peter who professed Jesus Christ, now says to him: 'You are the Christ, the Son of the living God. I will follow you, but let us not speak of the Cross. That has nothing to do with it. I will follow you on other terms, but without the Cross.' When we journey without the Cross, when we build without the Cross, when we confess Christ without the Cross, we are not disciples of the Lord, we are worldly: we may be bishops, priests, cardinals, popes, but not disciples of the Lord."

There was no doubt that Pope Francis was being "realistic," with the type of Christian realism that allowed the Gospel writers to keep all those passages that refer to Peter's betrayal of Christ, with the type of realism that understands how fallible all men are—the realism that says that each life will have its suffering, which must be faced and borne.

And then Pope Francis concluded this brief, dramatic homily with a prayer, a wish: "My wish," he said, "is that all of us, after these days of grace, will have the courage, yes, the courage, to walk in the presence of the Lord, with the Lord's Cross; to build the Church on the Lord's blood, which was poured out on the Cross; and to profess the one glory: Christ crucified. And in this way, the Church will go forward."

With these words, his homily came to an almost abrupt end. He wanted his fellow cardinals to show courage. He wanted them to "profess the one glory: Christ crucified" and not be concerned about worldly honor or financial ease. These were powerful, eloquent words, spoken simply and with real passion and conviction.

"My prayer for all of us is that the Holy Spirit, through the intercession of the Blessed Virgin Mary, our Mother, may grant us this grace," he concluded. "To walk, to build, to con-fess Jesus Christ crucified. So may it be."

In this sermon, Pope Francis did one thing that caught everyone's attention. He quoted not St. Augustine, or St. Thomas Aquinas, or even St. Francis or St. Ignatius, but a brilliant, controversial French Catholic convert from the late 1800s, Léon Bloy.

This citation was another important clue to the new pope's mind and heart. Francis was making clear his appreci-ation of this writer, who was among the most "politically in-correct" authors of all time, a man who came to be known as a "pilgrim of the Absolute" because of his uncompromising love of Christ. Bloy was the son of a Voltairean anti-Catholic and was raised as an agnostic. He converted to Catholicism in 1868 and decided to live a life of radical poverty, depend-ing completely upon charity.

His books are filled with memorable quotes such as: "Priests are latrines, they are there for humanity to pour out our filth" and "The worst evil is not the crime committed, but the failure to do the good one might have done." Because of his alleged intolerance, Bloy was hated by some of the leading French intellectuals of his time, such as Emile Zola, Guy de Maupassant, and Anatole France. But his radical Catholicism inspired a wave of conversions, including those of Georges Rouault, Maxence Van der Meersch, and the philosophers Jacques and Raissa Maritain.

Bloy was not only a furious polemicist and apologist, he was also a mystic who expressed himself with moving eloquence: "Love does not make you weak, because it is the source of all strength, but it makes you see the nothingness of the illusory strength on which you depended before you knew it."

Bloy longed for sainthood, for martyrdom, but saw himself as a sinner dependent on the mercy of God. This is an attitude that we see also in Pope Francis's life.

The remark the pope cites—"Anyone who does not pray to the Lord prays to the devil"—is certainly not politically correct. In fact, it is one of the most politically incorrect things the new pope could have quoted. We live in an increasingly "de-Christianized" age, when the figure of Christ, around whom Western culture for centuries was built, has increasingly been marginalized, even ostracized. So the attempt by Bloy, and by Francis in citing Bloy, to move Christ back to the enter of human attention, is a counterattack on this secularizing process. And Pope Francis cited Bloy in reference to the very activity that he had placed at the center of his first remarks from the balcony the previous evening: prayer.

"Anyone who does not pray to the Lord prays to the devil." That is, in the activity of prayer, in the moment that is so "beautiful" of praying, there is still a choice: to pray to the Lord, or to pray to the devil. Pope Francis, following Bloy, was setting forth a stark alternative: either Christ or the demonic.

We know that St. John writes of Christ as the Word of God, the *Logos* of God, and we know that *logos* means reason, means meaning itself. So, by extension, we understand Pope Francis to be saying, following Bloy, that there is only one reason, one meaning, one *logos* that can provide for man that clarity, that density of meaning that he craves—that absolute meaning. For Bloy, and for Pope Francis, that absolute *logos*, that pure meaning, is Christ. Anything other than Christ falls short of that pure meaning; that is, it is tinged with confusion and uncertainty, and it is eventually stained by that confusion until it becomes pure and absolute confusion, which is the demonic.

Pope Francis was pulling no punches. He was being entirely evangelical, entirely Christocentric. He was saying that "Christ is the only Savior" and that he is the only Savior "of all persons," in other words, of every human being, whether Christian or non-Christian, whether living in the Mediterranean area or in the farthest corner of the earth, whether living today, or in the past, or in the future. He was expressing a universal vision of Christ's salvific mission and work.

If the pope's trip across Rome in the early morning had been to express his devotion to Mary, his discourse to the cardinals that afternoon was a profession of an integral, unswerving faith in the Risen Christ. From the Marian spirituality expressed by his visit to St. Mary Major in the morning, we had come to the Christocentric spirituality of his late afternoon discourse to his cardinals.

Upon finishing his address, the pope personally greeted all the cardinals.

The Keys to the House

On Thursday evening—twenty-four hours after his election—Pope Francis received the keys to the papal apartments. Cardinal Tarcisio Bertone, seventy-eight, who served Pope Benedict XVI as secretary of state and was responsible as *camerlengo*, or chamberlain, during the *sede vacante*, for sealing the apartments, cut the red ribbon that sealed the doors, then gave the silver-colored key to the new pontiff.

The prefect of the papal household, Archbishop Georg Gänswein, then entered to give the pope a tour of his new home.

While the new pope stood by the door, looking into the blackness of the empty papal apartment, Archbishop Gänswein, also Pope Emeritus Benedict's personal secretary, seemed to hesitate. For a moment each man peered into the darkness. Gänswein then walked forward to find the light switch. He knew the way, because he had lived in this home for nearly eight years. He reached the far wall, touched the switch, and the apartments were lit.

Francis walked into the rooms that had been vacated just two weeks before by Benedict and were now reserved for him.

Gänswein's initial hesitation, his cautious walk into the dark, the patient waiting by the others, seemed to speak of the fragility of men in the flux of time and change. We see now as in a glass darkly, and only after this life will we see truly, and see as we are seen.

CHAPTER 4

....

First Meeting with His
Fellow Cardinals

MARCH 15: VISITING MEJÍA

Like good wine that improves with age, let us give the
youth the wisdom of our lives.
—*Pope Francis, speaking to the assembled cardinals of*
the Church on March 15, 2013

On the morning of his second full day as pope, Francis met with the College of Cardinals in the Apostolic Palace. There he delivered a remarkable address, which
turned into a reflection on old age. In the circumstances of
his election, after the decision of Pope Benedict to step down
at age eighty-five, Pope Francis seemed to be giving us an
insight into how he planned to treat Benedict, nine years his
senior.

Francis spoke about creating a "harmony" in the College
of Cardinals. His words echoed the words of Pope Benedict
on February 28, in his final meeting with the college before

his renunciation of the Petrine office. It seemed no accident that Francis, in his first meeting with the cardinals, echoed Benedict's words in his last.

"Courage, dear brothers!" Pope Francis began. "Probably half of us are in our old age. Old age, they say, is the seat of wisdom. The old ones have the wisdom that they have earned from walking through life. Like old Simeon and Anna at the temple whose wisdom allowed them to recognize Jesus. Let us give with wisdom to the youth: like good wine that improves with age, let us give the youth the wisdom of our lives."

Francis was addressing the entire College of Cardinals, both electors and nonelectors, in the Clementine Hall. He improvised several times during his talk—including when he informed them that Cardinal Jorge Mejía, ninety, also from Argentina, had suffered a heart attack two days before and was recovering at the Pius XI private clinic.

Before beginning his address, the pope listened to the greeting that Cardinal Angelo Sodano, dean of the College of Cardinals, read to him on behalf of the college.

"We give thanks to the Lord our God," Sodano began. "This is the liturgical invitation that we, the Cardinal Fathers, address to one another, between the 'seniors' and the 'juniors,' to thank the Lord for the gift that He has made to His Holy Church, giving us a new Shepherd. . . . Know, Holy Father, that all of us, your cardinals, are at your full disposal, seeking to build with you the apostolic cenacle of the nascent Church, the Upper Room of Pentecost. We will try to keep 'an open mind and a believing heart,' as you wrote in your book of meditations."

During his own address, Francis said that their meeting sought "to be almost an extension of the intense ecclesial communion experienced in this period. Enlivened by a profound sense of responsibility and supported by a great love for Christ and the Church, we have prayed together, sharing our fraternal feelings, our experiences and reflections. A mutual understanding and openness has grown in this climate of great cordiality. This is good because we are brothers."

A central point of his talk was to express his "great affection" and "profound gratitude" to "my venerable Predecessor Benedict XVI."

Pope Francis focused on the Christ-centeredness of Benedict's spirituality and pontificate. "The Petrine ministry, lived with total dedication," Francis said, "found in him a wise and humble exponent, his gaze always firmly on Christ, the risen Christ, present and alive in the Eucharist."

Then Francis spoke in a profound way about the action of the Holy Spirit. "Our acquaintance and mutual openness have helped us to be docile to the action of the Holy Spirit," Francis said. "He, the Paraclete, is the ultimate source of every initiative and manifestation of faith. . . . It is he who creates unity from differences, not in 'equality,' but in harmony. I remember the Father of the Church who described him thus: *'Ipse harmonia est'* [The Holy Spirit is harmony itself]. The Paraclete, who gives different charisms to each of us, unites us in this community of the Church."

These words are also very reminiscent of the words of Benedict on February 28. Benedict urged his cardinals to pray so that the College of Cardinals could be "like an orchestra," where diversity, as an expression of the Universal Church, always contributes to a higher sense of harmony. The Church, Pope Benedict stressed then, is a living body, "as was so clearly seen through the crowds gathered in St. Peter's Square for the last Wednesday general audience." Through the Church, Benedict said, the mystery of the Incarnation "remains forever present" so that "Christ continues to walk through all times and in all places."

The continuity between Benedict's final address and Francis's first became even clearer in Francis's actual citation of Pope Benedict.

Francis noted that "the period of the Conclave was full of meaning, not only for the College of Cardinals, but also for all the faithful. In these days we felt, almost tangibly, the affection and solidarity of the universal Church, as well as the attention of many people who, although they do not share our faith, look to the Church and the Holy See with respect and admiration."

Francis then continued: "I think with great affection and deep gratitude of my venerable predecessor, Benedict XVI, who during these years of his pontificate has enriched and strengthened the Church with his teaching, his goodness, his guidance, his faith, his humility, and his gentleness, which will remain a spiritual heritage for all."

He noted that, "as Pope Benedict XVI reminded us so often in his teachings and most recently with his brave and humble gesture, Christ is the one who guides the Church through His Spirit. The Holy Spirit is the soul of the Church, with his life-giving force that unifies one body from many: the mystical Body of Christ."

He went on, "Let us never give in to pessimism, to that bitterness that the devil offers us every day. Do not give in to pessimism and discouragement. We have the firm certainty that the Holy Spirit gives the Church with His mighty breath, the courage to persevere and also to seek new methods of evangelization, to bring the Gospel to the ends of the earth."

This was the second time in two days that Francis had spoken of "the evil one."

Then Francis used words reminiscent of the teaching of Don Luigi Giussani, founder of the Communion and Liberation movement, whose works Pope Francis has studied since the early 1990s.

The new pope said to his cardinals: "The Christian truth is attractive and persuasive because it responds to the deep needs of human existence, convincingly announcing that Christ is the only Savior of the whole person and of all persons. This announcement is as valid today as it was at the beginning of Christianity when there was a great missionary expansion of the Gospel."

Francis ended his talk by using an expression quite common in Pope Emeritus Benedict's teaching, that the "face of Christ" is what we desire to look upon, that the "beautiful face" of that person Christ, the splendor of that face, will be, in fact, the blessing of ultimate communion in eternity.

And this Christocentric quality to Pope Francis's discourse grew more acute in his final words: "Now, return to your Sees to continue your ministry, enriched by the experience of these days that have been so full of faith and ecclesial communion. This unique and incomparable experience has allowed us to understand in depth the beauty of ecclesial reality, which is a reflection of the splendor of the Risen Christ. One day we'll look upon that beautiful face of the Risen Christ."

So this discourse to his cardinals was a powerful call by Francis to the cardinals to "never give in to that bitterness the devil offers" and rather to seek always that "beautiful face"—speaking of Christ's beauty, not his goodness or his truthfulness, as his most "attractive" quality—which Francis said would be the face they all would see at the end of life's journey.

LATER THAT afternoon, in almost total secrecy, driving in an unmarked car, Pope Francis visited a Roman hospital where Cardinal Jorge Mejía was being cared for.

Francis, by going to visit with Mejía, once again showed his simplicity: no large entourage, no large number of body-guards, everything very low-key. The unplanned visit lasted about thirty minutes. It marked the pontiff's second public outing since being elected. After greeting the cardinal, the pope stopped at the hospital's chapel to pray with the thir-teen nuns of the San José de Gerona Order, who work in the hospital. He made it a point to speak individually with the nuns and with others who were in the chapel.

Controversies and Outreach

This second full day of the pontificate was marked by an outburst of allegations in the global press against then Cardinal Bergoglio. The charge: that he had "collaborated" with the military junta in Argentina during the 1970s, when an estimated thirty thousand government opponents were arrested, and many killed, by the regime.

Father Federico Lombardi, S.J., director of the Holy See Press Office, read a statement during the afternoon press conference responding to the allegations.

"The campaign against Bergoglio is well-known and dates back to many years ago," Father Lombardi began. The Vati-can press director then attacked the credibility of the source. The campaign, he said, "has been made by a publication that carries out sometimes slanderous and defamatory campaigns."

And he added, "The anticlerical cast of this campaign and of other accusations against Bergoglio is well-known and obvious."

Then Lombardi addressed the accusations themselves. He began by saying that the charges related to a period of time "before Jorge Mario Bergoglio became bishop [of Buenos Aires], when he was Provincial Superior of the Jesuits in Argentina."

The charges "accuse him of not having protected two priests who were kidnapped," Lombardi said, adding, "This was never a concrete or credible accusation in his regard. He was questioned by an Argentinian court as someone aware of the situation but never as a defendant. He has, in documented form, denied any accusations."

For the Vatican, the accusations had no basis in fact. Moreover, the truth of Bergoglio's activity was that he had helped to protect many people. Lombardi continued, "There have been many declarations demonstrating how much Bergoglio did to protect many persons at the time of the military dictatorship. . . . Bergoglio's role, once he became bishop, in promoting a request for forgiveness of the Church in Argentina for not having done enough at the time of the dictatorship is also well-known."

Lombardi said that the accusations were being made by "anticlerical elements" interested in attacking the Church. The accusations "must be firmly rejected," he concluded.

Francis Greets Rome's Jewish Community

On the second day of his papacy Pope Francis sent a letter to Dr. Riccardo Di Segni, chief rabbi of Rome, the oldest Jewish community of the Diaspora.

"On this day of my election as Bishop of Rome and Pastor of the Universal Church," the letter said, "I send you my cordial greetings, informing you that the solemn inauguration of my pontificate will take place on Tuesday, March 19.

"Trusting in the protection of the Most High, I strongly hope to be able to contribute to the progress of the relations that have existed between Jews and Catholics since Vatican Council II in a spirit of renewed collaboration and in service of a world that may always be more in harmony with the Creator's will."

Curial Posts

Also on his second day as pope, Pope Francis made a decision not to decide yet on what to do about changing the personnel of the Roman Curia. He did not reconfirm all of the curial posts that had been "zeroed out" by Benedict XVI's renunciation of the papal throne on February 28. From that date, there had literally been no heads of the Roman dicasteries. All served at the request of the reigning pontiff, and with no pope, they had no mandate to continue in office. All of the Roman Curia leadership—prefects of Vatican Congregations, presidents of Vatican Councils—needed either to be reconfirmed by Pope Francis, or replaced by other men the new pope might choose, in order for the daily government of the Church to resume. In the past, popes have traditionally reappointed all curial leaders within twenty-four hours of their election. But Francis did not do that on his first day in office. And this decision to refrain from acting drew attention. Francis was evidently going to take more time to reconfirm the curial leadership. But how much more time? Or was he going to quickly make a number of changes? No one knew. He had already shown he was capable of making surprising decisions by leaving the Vatican without a large escort to go to the Basilica of St. Mary Major, and by paying his own bill at the front desk of the Vatican residence where he had stayed. Would his decisions—or non-decisions—regarding his Curia also be surprising?

CHAPTER 5

....

First Meeting with Journalists

MARCH 16: "FOR THE POOR"

First of all I would say a prayer for our Bishop Emeritus Benedict XVI. Let us all pray together for him,
that the Lord bless him and Our Lady protect him.

—*Pope Francis, during his first public words*
after his election, March 13, 2013

On the third day of his pontificate, March 16, it
was officially announced that Pope Francis would
go to Castel Gandolfo, about fifteen miles outside of Rome,
to meet Pope Emeritus Benedict on March 23. This would
be the long-awaited first meeting of two popes in history.
According to a Vatican communiqué, Pope Francis would
leave by helicopter from the Vatican at noon and arrive at
12:15 P.M. at Castel Gandolfo, where he would join the pope
emeritus for lunch.

Pope Francis had already rendered homage to Pope
Emeritus Benedict on several occasions, beginning with a
telephone call on the night of his election. Then, standing

on the balcony of St. Peter's, Francis asked the crowd below to pray for Benedict. On Friday, at the meeting with his cardinals, Francis recalled the "goodness" of his predecessor, and referred to his decision to step down as a "courageous and humble" gesture.

One difference between Benedict and his successor had already become evident. Pope Francis was not wearing the "red shoes" that past popes have typically worn. This tradition goes back more than two hundred years. It has no doctrinal significance, of course. But it is a tradition. And Francis, so far, is not following it. Since his election, Francis has worn an ordinary pair of black shoes.

Benedict's red shoes were handmade for him by a cobbler in the Borgo, the old area of medieval streets just next to the Vatican on the side of St. Peter's Square. A pair of the red shoes had been made for his successor and were on display in the days before the conclave.

But Pope Francis had instead worn his old black shoes. Reports say that before he left Buenos Aires for Rome, Cardinal Bergoglio was wearing shoes so shabby that friends insisted on buying him a new pair. "He's always very humbly dressed, and the shoes he was wearing were not in very good shape," a South American priest told Vatican Radio.

The *New York Times* commented: "[Francis] wore simple black shoes and an ordinary wristwatch with a thick black band to his first Mass as pontiff. . . . In an ancient institution where style often translates into substance, Francis, in his first twenty-four hours as Pope, has dramatically shifted the tone of the papacy. Whereas Benedict XVI, the pope emeritus, was a theologian who favored red loafers, ermine-lined cloaks, and erudite homilies, reviving papal fashions from centuries past, Francis, the former Cardinal Jorge Mario

Bergoglio of Buenos Aires, appeared Thursday to be sending a message of radical humility."

The Love of the Poor as a Central Christian Mission

This matter of red shoes and black shoes is not simply a matter of taste, or even of a desire for simplicity. Pope Francis is showing us his "program" by such small gestures.

It is to set the love of the poor and downtrodden and miserable and despairing at the heart of the mission of the pope, of the Church hierarchy, of the Church as a whole, and so, of individual Christians. The pope is telling us that, to be Christians, to bear witness to the love of Christ, to the reality of Christ and his love for us, shown in his life and his willingness to lay down his life for us on the cross, we must show our love for the poor and the downtrodden in real, practical, evident ways.

And he made this very clear in his meeting with the five thousand members of the press who are in Rome. On the third day after his election, Francis agreed—as has become customary, so in this he kept to tradition—to meet with the press.

Once again he departed from written text, and told the group why he had chosen the name Francis. And why this choice will mark his pontificate.

"Do you know why the Bishop of Rome wanted to be called Francis?" he asked.

> During the papal election, I had at my side the Archbishop Emeritus of São Paulo, Cardinal Cláudio Hummes. A great friend, a great friend....

When things began to be a little dangerous, he comforted me! And when the votes arrived at two-thirds, and when the cardinals began to applaud in their customary way because the pope had been elected, he put his arms around me, he hugged me, and he said to me: "Never forget the poor."

This word stayed with me, the poor, the poor. And after that, thinking about the poor, I thought of St. Francis of Assisi. And then, while the vote counting continued, I thought about war, until the end of the voting. And Francis is the man of peace. And it was thus that the name Francis came to me in my heart, Francis of Assisi. The man of poverty, the man of peace, the man who loved.

The pope paused for a moment and added: "How I wish for a Church that is poor, and for the poor!"

There were also beautiful words in this talk about the Church. The pope stressed that the Church does not have a "political" nature but is essentially something "spiritual." And he stressed the centrality of Christ, not the pope, for the Church. "Christ is the center!" he said. "Without Him, Peter and the Church would not exist and would have no reason to exist."

In this context, he spoke about Pope Benedict's decision to renounce the papal throne. "As Benedict XVI frequently reminded us, Christ is present in the Church and guides her," Pope Francis said. "In everything that has occurred, the principal agent has been, in the final analysis, the Holy Spirit. He prompted the decision of Benedict XVI for the good of the Church; He guided the cardinals in prayer and in the election." This, he summed up, was the key to understanding the events of recent days.

And then Francis did something that surprised everyone, pleased many, and shocked a few.

The moment had come for him to impart his apostolic blessing, but he did not do this in the usual way. In fact, he made no exterior gesture at all. He did not lift his hand, he did not move it in the sign of the cross, and he did not speak "in the name of the Father, and of the Son, and of the Holy Spirit" out loud.

He said, in Italian: "I cordially impart to all of you my blessing. Thank you." And then, in Spanish, he explained: "I told you I was cordially imparting my blessing. Since many of you are not members of the Catholic Church, and others are not believers, I cordially give this blessing silently, to each of you, respecting the conscience of each, but in the knowledge that each of you is a child of God. May God bless you!"

And with that, he turned and left.

One of my colleagues turned to me and said, "Where was the papal blessing?"

"He gave it silently," I said. "He blessed us silently, without presupposing anything. He was trying to be respectful of individual consciences. This is not a purely religious gathering."

"But it still seems like something is missing," my friend said. "No blessing!"

"But there was a blessing," I said. "We just could not see it. It is like what Ratzinger used to say, that in heaven, in the presence of God, there will no longer be any external rites or rituals to signify our worship, all those things will pass away, because the perfect will have come."

"But are we already in heaven?" my friend replied.

"No," I said. "But can't we believe we are on the way?"

My friend was still not satisfied. "I would have liked to have received a blessing from him," he said.

"You did," I said.

Pope Francis, in his simple way, provided all of us with inspiration for meditation and a call to an inward conversion.

And that is what should be our thought at this time, just as Cardinal Cláudio Hummes told Pope Francis as the vote total rose: "Never forget the poor." We should never forget our own need for conversion. We should be converted to Christ. We are ever in need of deeper conversion. This is what Pope Francis is calling us to, if we can but hear him.

Curia Officials Reappointed— but Only "Temporarily"

An important decision was announced later that day. Pope Francis reconfirmed all the heads of the Vatican Curia offices. But he did so only *"donec aliter provideatur"* ("until otherwise it may be provided" or "until other decisions are taken" or, perhaps most simply, "just for now").

And in taking this decision, Francis was following tradition. All new popes restore their curial officials a day or two after their election, so that the Curia, which is "zeroed out" at the departure of one pope, can be restored to a functioning body.

He followed tradition—but the phrasing of the decision means that he is leaving the door open to radical personnel changes in the Curia. If he does not take such decisions within a few weeks, or months, that would suggest there is not going to be a "clean sweep" of the Curia. The future remains to be seen.

CHAPTER 6

·····························

First Parish Mass

MARCH 17: AT THE CHURCH OF
ST. ANNE, THE MOTHER OF MARY

He comes for us when we recognize that we are sinners. . . . This is the Lord's most powerful message:
mercy.

—*Pope Francis*

On his first Sunday as pope, the fourth full day of his
papacy, Pope Francis celebrated Mass in St. Anne's
Church, the tiny parish church of Vatican City, not in St. Peter's Basilica (this was because he had not yet been installed).

When the pope arrived at the church, he received applause. Before going inside, he paused to greet the many
worshipers present, shaking hands, blessing children in their
parents' arms, treating a group of Argentinians to an un-
scripted exchange. Then, to the consternation of his security
guards, he walked a few steps toward the Porta Sant'Anna
and continued right out of the Vatican into the street in front
of the gate, where a large crowd was waiting. A few minutes

were spent greeting people behind the barriers. Once again, he had shown that he was a "pope of the people," desirous of being near people, not distant from them.

The Gospel reading for the day was from St. John, the story of the woman caught in adultery. Under Jewish law, she was subject to execution by stoning. But when the woman was presented to Jesus for judgment, Jesus said, "Let he among you who is without sin cast the first stone."

Mercy was the key lesson, mercy was the "Good News" proclaimed this Sunday, Francis said. "Mercy," he said, "is the Lord's most powerful message."

Speaking without a prepared text, Pope Francis said, "If we are like the Pharisee before the altar [who said], 'Thank you, Lord, for not making me like all the other men, and especially not like that fellow at the door, like that publican,' well, then we do not know the heart of the Lord, and we shall not ever have the joy of feeling this mercy."

Pope Francis was adamant: "It is not easy to entrust one-self to God's mercy," he said, "because it is an abyss beyond our comprehension. But we must!"

He then gave snippets of vaguely remembered conversation with someone about this mercy, significantly revealing much about his own pastoral compassion.

"Oh, Father," he said, speaking in the place of a person coming to him for spiritual help, "if you knew my life, you would not say that to me!"

"Why, what have you done?" the pope continued, re-counting this conversation.

"Oh, I am a great sinner!" he went on, in the voice of the penitent.

"All the better!" the pope continued, in the voice of the priest. "Go to Jesus: he likes you to tell him these things!"

One could sense in these words the style of Pope Francis's spiritual direction: he is generous with God's forgiveness, generous with the forgiveness of Christ—just as Christ was generous with his forgiveness to the woman taken in adultery.

"He forgets," the pope said, speaking of Christ. "He has a very special capacity for forgetting. He forgets, he kisses you, he embraces you, and he simply says to you: 'Neither do I condemn you; go, and sin no more.' That is the only advice he gives you. After a month, if we are in the same situation, let us go back to the Lord. The Lord never tires of forgiving: never! It is we who tire of asking his forgiveness."

And he concluded with two very powerful sentences that seemed to express the essence of his pastoral spirituality: "Let us ask for the grace not to tire of asking forgiveness, because he never tires of forgiving. Let us ask for this grace."

And so the unusual mass at the local Vatican parish church became the occasion for an unusual, very simple, very pastoral, papal sermon, one accessible to all—a mark of many of this pope's actions and gestures in his first days as pope.

Greeting for Father Gonzalo

After Mass and after greeting the parish priest and Cardinal Angelo Comastri, the Vatican official in charge of St. Peter's Basilica, the pope concluded with these words:

There are some here who are not parishioners, including a few from Argentina—one is my Auxiliary Bishop—but today they are parishioners. I want to introduce to you a priest who comes from far away, a priest who works with children and with drug addicts on the street. He opened a school for them; he has

done many things to make Jesus known, and all those
boys and girls off the street, they today work with the
studies they have done; they have the ability to work,
they believe and they love Jesus. I ask you, [Father]
Gonzalo [indicating the priest], to come greet the
people. Pray for him. He works in Uruguay; he is the
founder of Jubilar Juan Pablo II. This is his work. I
do not know how he came here, but I will find out!
Thanks. Pray for him.

In Pope Francis's home city, when he saw young people
experimenting with crack cocaine and slowly destroying their
lives, he blazed with a righteous fury because of his deep
love for these young people. He denounced drug dealing—
especially of the drug *paco*, a form of crack cocaine processed
with sulfuric acid and kerosene that quickly destroyed the
beautiful, healthy minds of so many young people. In 2011,
Bergoglio condemned child trafficking and sex slavery in
Buenos Aires, saying, "In this city, there are many girls who
stop playing with dolls to enter the dump of a brothel because they were stolen, sold, betrayed. . . . In this city, women
and girls are kidnapped, and they are subjected to use and
abuse of their body; they are destroyed in their dignity. The
flesh that Jesus assumed and died for is worth less than the
flesh of a pet. A dog is cared for better than these slaves of
ours, who are kicked, who are broken" (*La Nacion*, September
24, 2011, citing Bergoglio's homily at the fourth Mass for the
Victims of Human Trafficking, Buenos Aires).

Once again, as on every other day of his papacy, Pope
Francis emphasized prayer, asked for prayer, this time not
for himself but for a priest faced with many problems as he
works with drug addicts in Uruguay.

CHAPTER 7

....

First Angelus

Have a good Sunday, and have a good lunch!
—*Pope Francis*

At noon on Sunday, St. Peter's Square was packed. At least 150,000 people were present, according to the estimate of the director of the Vatican press office, Father Federico Lombardi, S.J., to hear Pope Francis's first Angelus.

"Brothers and sisters, good day," Pope Francis began. "After our first meeting last Wednesday, I am again able to greet you all and am happy to do so on Sunday, the Lord's day. It's good for Christians to speak and exchange greetings on Sunday and today we do so in a square to which the media have given a global dimension."

These were the first public words of the new pontiff, and they were met by a roar.

He spoke only in Italian, omitting the traditional greetings in other languages.

Pope Francis told two jokes during his talk, winning more hearts. On a more serious note, he continued to ask people to never get tired of asking God for forgiveness.

"Don't forget this, the Lord never gets tired of forgiving, it is we that get tired of asking forgiveness," Pope Francis said. "Let us not hear or condone words of contempt, but only words of love and mercy that invite us to conversion."

The new pope said that the face of God is like that of a merciful father who always has patience and is always willing to forgive us. "Have you thought about how much patience he has with you?" he asked.

Pope Francis told how he recently read a book by German cardinal Walter Kasper, who is considered in Catholic circles to be a slightly more "liberal" theologian than his fellow countryman Pope Emeritus Benedict XVI (so Pope Francis's mention of him raised eyebrows), on mercy.

"That book has done me so much good, but don't think I'm trying to make publicity of my cardinals!" Francis said. "It's not like that! It's done me so much good because he says that mercy changes everything, it changes the world, making it less cold and more fair."

Pope Francis also told a story about how, when the image of Our Lady of Fatima arrived in Buenos Aires in 1992, when he was bishop, a large Mass was celebrated for the poor, and he was hearing confessions. He had a conversation with "an old and very humble lady" who came to him toward the end of the Mass. The Catholic News Agency organized the story as a simple dialogue:

Pope:	Nonna, do you want to confess yourself?
Woman:	Yes.
Pope:	But you haven't sinned.
Woman:	We've all sinned.
Pope:	But maybe God won't forgive you.
Woman:	God forgives everyone.
Pope:	How do you know, madame?
Woman:	If God didn't forgive everything, the world wouldn't exist.

Francis continued, laughing: "I wanted to ask her, 'Have you studied at the Gregorian [University]?' because that is the knowledge that the Holy Spirit gives!"

Pope Francis then extended his greetings to all the faithful and said he chose the name Francis to spiritually tie himself to Italy, the country his family is originally from. "But Jesus has called us to form part of a new family of his Church, in this family of God walking together on the path of the Gospel," he said.

Pope Francis ended his first Angelus prayer wishing everyone "a good Sunday and a good lunch."

Afterward, the pope greeted the tens of thousands of faithful who overflowed St. Peter's Square: "Thank you for your welcome and your prayers," he said.

I ask that you pray for me. I renew my embrace to the faithful of Rome and extend it to all of you who have come from various parts of Italy and the world just as to those who are joining in with us by means of the media. I have chosen the name of the Patron Saint of Italy, St. Francis of Assisi, and this reinforces my spiritual ties to this land that, as you

know, is where my family originated. But Jesus has
called us to be part of a new family: his Church. [He
has called] this family of God to walk together the
paths of the Gospel. May the Lord bless you and the
Virgin protect you! And don't forget this: The Lord
never tires of forgiving. We are the ones who tire of
asking forgiveness.

Francis's First Papal Tweet

Pope Francis issued his first tweet that Sunday, shortly
after performing his first Angelus prayer, with a consistent message: "Pray for me."

"Dear friends, I thank you from my heart and ask you
to continue to pray for me," he tweeted from the @Pontifex
account.

Jesuit Father General on His Visit with the Pope

Pope Francis and Adolfo Nicolás, S.J., superior general
of the Society of Jesus, met at the Domus Santa Marta.
This account was written by the father general himself.

Visit with Pope Francis of March 17

At the personal invitation of Pope Francis, I went to
the Santa Marta House, which had been used for the
Cardinals present at the Conclave, at 5:30 P.M. He was
at the entrance and received me with the usual Jesuit
embrace. We had a few pictures taken, at his request,
and at my apologies for not keeping protocol he insisted that I treat him like any other Jesuit, at the *tu*

level, so I did not have to worry about treatments, "Holiness" or "Holy Father."

I offered him all our Jesuit resources because in his new position he is going to need counsel, thinking, persons, et cetera. He showed gratitude for this and at the invitation to visit us for lunch at the Curia he said he would oblige.

There was full commonality of feeling on several issues that we discussed and I remained with the conviction that we will work very well together for the service of the Church in the name of the Gospel.

There was calm, humor, and mutual understanding about past, present, and future. I left the place with the conviction that it will be worth cooperating fully with him in the Vineyard of the Lord. At the end he helped me with my coat and accompanied me to the door. That added a couple of salutes to me from the Swiss Guards there. A Jesuit embrace, again, is a good way to meet and send off a friend.

ALSO ON this day in Rome was a talented young American writer Kathryn Jean Lopez, editor-at-large of *National Review Online* and a director of Catholic Voices USA. She offered a few lines of thoughtful reflection on the new pope, and memorably described Pope Francis's voice when he spoke to the world as a "soft whisper of love."

He's a Latin American with Italian roots, who studied in Germany. . . . As a Jesuit he's a member of a truly international religious community, and his ties to *Comunione e Liberazione* make him part of another global network. Those different strands he can tie together.

Communion and Liberation has helped people encounter Christ and engage the culture—two leading
messages of Pope Benedict XVI's papacy, which he
stressed in his final days. . . . He may not have been the
pundits' pick, but he was not a long-shot pick, having
been in the running last time around. And that he is
both a Jesuit and close to a movement, where resides
much of the lifeblood of the renewal of the Church, is
powerful. I enjoy a bit that I and most every prognosti-
cator was wrong. . . .

The other night the first thing I did when I got to
St. Peter's on Sunday was go to Confession. My confessor handed me a St. Francis holy card. [The prayer
on the card] could easily be an ecumenical prayer that
Pope Francis and those he shepherds pray and live. . . .
A friend described Francis's voice over the Square, to
the world, tonight as a "soft whisper of love." How the
world could use such a soothing sound from someone
whose witness offers us a challenge.

CHAPTER 8

First Explanation of His Vocation: Francis's Coat of Arms

"Miserando atque Eligendo"

We cannot understand this dynamic of encounter which brings forth wonder and adherence if it has not been triggered—forgive me the use of this word—by mercy. Only someone who has encountered mercy, who has been caressed by the tenderness of mercy, is happy and comfortable with the Lord. I beg the theologians who are present not to turn me in to the Sant'Uffizio or to the Inquisition; however, forcing things a bit, I dare to say that the privileged locus of the encounter with the Lord is the caress of the mercy of Jesus Christ on my sin.

—*Cardinal Jorge Bergoglio, Buenos Aires,*
April 27, 2001, presentation of a book by Don
Luigi Giussani, L'attrattiva Gesù

In these words, Pope Francis, when he was still Cardinal Bergoglio, spoke about the mysterious subject of human sin and divine mercy. Of course, in a world in which the belief in the divine has often seemed almost to flicker out, like a candle with no more wax to nourish it, to speak of human sin and divine forgiveness is to speak of something incomprehensible. None of the terms, not *sin*, not *forgiveness*, not *divine*, and, arguably, not even *human* any longer makes much sense to modern Western men and women. And yet, for Bergoglio, they did make sense. Why? Because he had experienced the reality that these words signify: the reality of his own sin, the reality, therefore, of his imperfection, of his fallenness, of his misery, and being someone he did not want to be, and doing things he did not want to do—the reality of being a sinner. And he had also experienced forgiveness, mercy, the mercy that could actually look directly upon his sin, even embrace that sin (he uses the word *caress*), and then forgive that sin. And for Bergoglio, this was critical; it was the pivot point around which his life, his understanding of his calling, his understanding of his mission, turned.

For, as he said, "only someone who has encountered mercy, who has been caressed by the tenderness of mercy, is happy and comfortable with the Lord." In other words, the experience of forgiveness is required to "meet" the Lord, that is, Jesus, the Savior, the one who could forgive, the one who does forgive. In short, becoming a Christian, becoming a follower of Christ, becoming someone who is "in relationship with Christ," depends on encountering the mercy of Christ.

And one encounters that mercy because one needs that mercy, one is desperate—"without hope"—if one cannot find that mercy, that forgiveness, that healing from the woundedness and alienation that sin brings. Because sin alienates one from oneself. One wishes to do the good, to be true, to be drawn toward the beautiful, and one instead does the bad, is false, unfaithful, and is drawn—against one's own will, in a sense—toward what is ugly. So there is a chasm in our hearts, a wound, which is the cause of sin, and the result of sin, and which must be healed if we are to become reconciled to ourselves, to be made whole, to be filled with peace.

"The privileged locus of the encounter with the Lord is the caress of the mercy of Jesus Christ on my sin," Bergoglio said, in an astonishing phrase.

I am reminded of the equally astonishing statement of the great English mystic Julian of Norwich (1342–1416). At about the age of thirty, suffering from a grave illness and believing she was dying, Julian for several weeks had a series of intense visions of Jesus Christ. These visions are the source of her major work, *Sixteen Revelations of Divine Love.*

In her book, she speaks of God's love in terms of joy, compassion, and forgiveness as opposed to law, duty, and condemnation. She also believed that sin is, in a certain sense, "necessary" in life because it brings self-knowledge leading to acceptance of the role of God in one's life. The pain caused by sin, she believed, is an earthly reminder of the pain of the passion of Christ. Therefore, as people suffer as Christ did, they will become closer to him.

She claimed that her most famous saying, "All shall be well, and all shall be well, and all manner of thing shall be well," had been spoken to her by God himself.

I mention Julian of Norwich because of the extraordinary phrasing of Cardinal Bergoglio's reference to the "privileged locus" on the "encounter" with Christ: in "the caress of the mercy of Jesus Christ on my sin."

Now most of the time in Catholic teaching and theology, sin is regarded with such horror and hatred—"love the sinner, hate the sin"—that to speak of "caressing" a sin seems shocking. And, in fact, Bergoglio recognized this, saying,

"I beg the theologians who are present not to turn me in to the Sant'Uffizio or to the Inquisition." But he felt compelled to continue, to "force things a bit," because he had something profound that he wanted to communicate, and he was willing to risk even the appearance of heterodoxy to express this truth.

In the end, this is the most important truth of all. The truth about meeting Christ. Given the fact that human beings sin, and in so doing alienate ourselves from both ourselves and God, we must be forgiven, we must be shown mercy, or every single human being would be unable to be "righteous" and stand in the presence of the holy God.

And in our misery, in our longing to be healed, and made whole, and no longer miserable but joyful, human beings need to meet the "holy one" who can communicate his holiness, his mercy, his righteousness, his very life to them, and so save them.

The distance is so great between sin and holiness that what is required is the action, first of all, of God. God must come toward us and save us. This was all implied in these few words of Cardinal Bergoglio.

The encounter is necessary. The encounter is desired. The encounter is salutary, it is saving. But it cannot occur without God's mercy, without his love, without his love of the person even who has sinned and fallen, without "the caress of his mercy on my sin."

Why have I gone so deeply into this one small statement?

Because Pope Francis had personally experienced what he was talking about in this passage. And if we would wish to know this pope intimately, we must know this about him. We must know that he had experienced "the caress of the mercy of Christ," even, and especially, on his sin, and in that place, he had encountered the Lord and given his entire life to him.

We know this for a very simple reason: the Vatican told us about it in a press release. But strangely, almost no other writer has read the press release as I have read it. It is as if there is a resistance to speaking about something so intimate as the conversion and salvation of a soul. Because that is what we are speaking about here.

On the morning of March 18, the Vatican presented Pope Francis's coat of arms and the motto he had chosen from St. Bede, *"Miserando atque eligendo."* The Vatican said this:

THE SHIELD

Pope Francis has decided to keep the essential elements of his earlier coat of arms, chosen at the time of his episcopal consecration and essentially a simple one.

The blue shield is surmounted by the symbols of pontifical dignity, the same as the one used by his predecessor, Benedict XVI [mitre and between keys in gold and silver, with a red cord]. Standing out above is the emblem of the Pope's Order, the Jesuits or Company of Jesus: a flaming sun with letters in red, *IHS*, the monogram of Christ. The letter *H* includes a cross; this has three nails in black immediately below it.

Below is a star and a grape-like plant [nard]. The star, according to ancient heraldic tradition, represents the Virgin Mary, mother of Christ and the Church; the other plant, which flowers like a lily, represents St. Joseph, patron of the Universal Church. In Spanish iconographic tradition, St. Joseph carries what looks like a lily in his hands. By including these images on his shield, the Pope has understood how best to display his devotion to Our Lady and to St. Joseph.

The Motto

The Holy Father, Francis's motto comes from a homily by the Venerable Bede, a priest (Om. 21; CCL 122, 149–151), commenting on the Gospel passage of St. Matthew's call, where he writes *"Vidit ergo Iesus publicanum et quia miserando atque eligendo vidit, ait illi: 'Sequere me'"* (Jesus saw a publican, looking upon him with love and choosing him, said to him: "Follow me").

The homily is a tribute to Divine Mercy and can be found in the Liturgy of the Hours for St. Matthew's feast day. It takes on a special role in the spiritual life of the Pope. In fact, on the Feast of St. Matthew, September 21, in the year 1953, the young Jorge Mario Bergoglio experienced, at the age of seventeen years, in a very special way, the loving presence of God in his life. Following a confession, he felt his heart touched and sensed the descent of the mercy of God, who with a look of tender love, called him to the religious life, following the example of St. Ignatius of Loyola.

When chosen as a Bishop, Bishop Bergoglio recalled this moment of the beginning of his special consecration in the Church and decided to choose St. Bede's expression as his motto and programme for life: *"Miserando atque eligendo"* (He showed mercy on him and called him), which is now in the Papal Coat of Arms.

The Mystical Experience

Why is Pope Francis so simple, so genuine, so evidently filled with the love of Christ? Part of the answer may be because God actually filled him with his love. Part of the answer may lie in this seemingly mystical experience.

One of the central claims of the Catholic faith is not only that God exists, that he is real, but also that he can communicate with human beings, that human beings can be "pierced" by the actual sense of the divine presence, can experience and be aware of this real presence, can—as the very first verse of the old Baltimore Catechism taught—"know" God, then "love and serve Him."

In fact, "the more we love God and enter into intimate contact with Him through prayer, the more He makes Himself known and enflames our hearts with His love," Pope Emeritus Benedict XVI explained on January 12, 2011, at one of his Wednesday general audiences, speaking on the possibility of true communion, true mystical union, with God.

Thus, Christianity holds that contact with God, communication with God, communion with God, is possible. It isn't an illusion. It can actually happen. And moreover, it happened to Pope Francis, at a certain time and place. This pope, at the age of seventeen, while deep in prayer, was touched by God. And that experience was at the origin of this pope's religious life—of the life he has lived from that day to this, of the life that has brought him to the See of Peter.

We know that many young people (perhaps all young people) pass through a period when they seek with great intensity to know their place in this world—to hear their calling, to find their true vocation. And now we know that Pope Francis passed through this same process. And this is another reason that the word *prayer*, and actually praying, are so important to him. Because this experience came in, and through, and after, prayer, much prayer, much anguish of heart and mind, as he sought the face of God and God's mercy.

Let's reexamine this story and try to understand it thoroughly.

We are told of an experience in which young Jorge felt his heart "touched" and "sensed" the "descent of the mercy of God." He felt, "in a very special way," the "loving presence of God in his life." He felt as if God were gazing upon him "with a look of tender love." These are all the elements of a personal experience of Christ (for Christ is God, and Christ is God's mercy). These are all the elements of a mystical, life-transforming experience of God's actual presence.

And it is significant that this experience occurred on the Feast of St. Matthew. In the Jewish world of the time of Christ, no one was more shunned than a publican, a Jew collecting taxes from his own people for the Roman authorities and making a large personal profit. Publicans were not allowed to trade, eat, or even pray with other Jews.

One day, while Matthew was counting his money, Jesus looked at him and said two words: "Follow me." Matthew rose, leaving his pieces of silver, to follow Christ. Matthew's original name, Levi, in Hebrew means "adhesion." His new name, Matthew, means "gift of God." Matthew is also mentioned in the Gospels as the host of a dinner party for Christ and his companions to which Matthew invited his fellow tax collectors. The Jews were surprised to see Jesus with a publican, but Jesus explained that he had come "not to call the just, but sinners."

Matthew is known to us principally as the writer of one of the four Gospels—his Gospel is the first in the New Testament. Matthew's Gospel is believed to have been written in Aramaic, the language that Jesus spoke, and it was written to convince the Jews that their anticipated Messiah had come in the person of Jesus.

All of this relates to why Pope Francis is so open to those who are outside the Church—because he wishes to bring them in, as Matthew was brought in. He does not want anything that he does to exclude them. He wants to call to them, he wants them to hear his call, so that they, like Matthew, can see Christ and follow, beginning a new life.

St. Ignatius Loyola, the founder of the Jesuits, after having been gravely wounded in battle, had a vision that seems to have been an encounter with God as he really is, so that all creation acquired for him a new meaning and relevance, an experience that enabled Ignatius to "find God in all things" (the essential principle of Ignatian spirituality).

So the Jesuit Pope Francis, after much prayer, after confession and absolution, also experienced something extraordinary. For Ignatius, it was a vision; for Pope Francis, it was "the descent of the mercy of God." And nothing ever after was the same for him.

Reaction of Jewish Leaders, Groups

Soon after Francis was elected, we came to know that he was much loved and respected by Jewish leaders in Buenos Aires, and around the world.

"Jewish leaders around the world welcomed Wednesday's selection of Cardinal Jorge Mario Bergoglio as the pope of the Roman Catholic Church," wrote Jonah Lowenfeld in JewishJournal.com.

"In the Jewish community in Buenos Aires, the widely shared impression is that he's very friendly, that the cardinal was determined to have a cordial relationship with the Jewish community," Rabbi Marvin Hier, the dean and founder of the Simon Wiesenthal Center, said. Bergoglio had twice attended services at synagogues in Buenos Aires, Hier said, and had led a commemoration of the anniversary of Kristallnacht in his cathedral in December 2012.

Hier and other Jewish leaders were particularly encouraged by Bergoglio's reaction to the terrorist attack on a Jewish community center that killed more than eighty people. "We are heartened by his profound statement of solidarity with the Jewish people and his identity with the pain that was caused by the 1994 bombing of the AMIA Jewish center in Buenos Aires," Jewish Council for Public Affairs chair Larry Gold said in a statement immediately after Francis's election.

Rabbi Sergio Bergman, the senior rabbi of one of the largest synagogues in Buenos Aires and a member of the city's legislature since 2011, heralded Bergoglio's selection on Twitter. World Jewish Congress president Ronald S. Lauder, who met Bergoglio in 2008, expressed optimism that Francis would continue the work of building relationships between the Catholic Church and world Jewry. "He always had an open ear for our concerns," Lauder said. "I am sure that Francis will continue to be a man of dialogue, a man who is able to build bridges with other faiths."

Pope Francis has not said much publicly about Israel in the past, but Hier said he is hopeful that Francis will emerge as a supporter of the Jewish state. "We very much see him as a pope in the tradition of John Paul II and John XXIII," Hier said. John Paul II established formal relations between the Vatican and Israel in 1993.

In fact, Francis was on such good terms with the Jewish community of Buenos Aires that he spent hours over the past couple of years with Rabbi Abraham Skorka, rector of the Latin American Rabbinical Seminary. The two men talked about a wide range of subjects, including some very personal matters. There seems to be no doubt that this relationship reveals a profound respect between the two men, and so between two leaders of the Catholic and Jewish communities of Argentina.

"Dazzled" by a Girl

One thing the conversations with Rabbi Skorka reveal is that, even after his profound mystical experience, Bergoglio's life path wasn't without "temptations." And this too is a key thing to know about Pope Francis: He had the ordinary life of a young man, he experienced the ordinary feelings of young people, including the desire to get married and have a family—partly because his childhood experience of family had been so warm and supportive.

Bergoglio told Rabbi Skorka:

> When I was a seminarian, I was dazzled by a girl I met at an uncle's wedding. I was surprised by her beauty, her intellectual brilliance . . . and, well, I was bowled over for quite a while. I kept thinking and thinking about her.
>
> When I returned to the seminary after the wedding, I could not pray for over a week because, when I tried to do so, the girl appeared in my head. I had to rethink what I was doing. I was still free because I was a seminarian, so I could have gone back home and that was it. I had to think about my choice again.
>
> I chose again—or let myself be chosen by—the religious path.

So, for a least a brief time, Pope Francis thought of leaving the seminary and of not being ordained as a priest. "It would be abnormal for this kind of thing not to happen," he told Skorka. And he added, acknowledging that seminarians can feel that they are no longer called to the priesthood: "When this happens, one has to get one's bearings again. It's a matter of one choosing again or saying, 'No, what I'm feeling is very beautiful. I am afraid I won't be faithful to my commitment later on, so I'm leaving the seminary.'"

Before being a bishop in charge of a diocesan seminary, and before being a former director of formation for the Jesuit province of Argentina, Bergoglio had experienced these crises. And his words to Rabbi Skorka show his realism, and compassion: "When something like this happens to a seminarian, I help him go in peace to be a good Christian and not a bad priest." His words also show that he has reflected deeply on the question of priestly celibacy, and on how Christians over the centuries have treated this discipline. "In the Western Church to which I belong," Bergoglio said, "priests cannot be married as in the Byzantine, Ukrainian, Russian, or Greek Catholic Churches. In those Churches, the priests can be married, but the bishops have to be celibate. They are very good priests. Sometimes I joke with them and tell them that they have wives at home but they did not realize that they also got a mother-in-law as part of the bargain."

He continued:

In Western Catholicism, some organizations are pushing for more discussion about the issue. For now, the discipline of celibacy stands firm. Some say, with a certain pragmatism, that we are losing manpower. If, hypothetically, Western Catholicism were to review the issue of celibacy, I think it would do so for cultural reasons (as in the East), not so much as a universal option.

For the moment, I am in favor of maintaining celibacy, with all its pros and cons, because we have ten centuries of good experiences rather than failures.

What happens is that the scandals have an immediate impact. Tradition has weight and validity. Catholic ministers chose celibacy little by little. Up until 1100, some chose it and some did not. After that, the East followed the tradition of noncelibacy as personal choice, while the West went the opposite way. It is a matter of discipline, not of faith. It can change. Personally, it never crossed my mind to marry. But there are cases. Look at the case of the Paraguayan President, Fernando Lugo. He's a brilliant man. But as a bishop, he had a fall and resigned from his diocese. This decision was honest. Sometimes we see priests fall into this.

Rabbi Skorka asked Bergoglio: "And what is your position then?"

"If one of my priests comes and tells me that he got a woman pregnant, I listen," Bergoglio said. "I try to help him have peace and little by little I try to help him realize that the natural law takes priority over his priesthood. So, he has to leave the ministry and should take care of that child, even if he chooses not to marry that woman. For just as that child has the right to have a mother, he has a right to the face of a father. I commit myself to arranging all the paperwork for him in Rome, but he has to leave everything. Now, if a priest tells me he got excited and that he had a fall, I help him to get on track again. There are priests who get on track again, and others who do not. Some, unfortunately, do not even tell their bishop."

Skorka asked: "What does it mean to get back on track?"

"To do penance, to keep their celibacy," Bergoglio replied. "The double life is no good for us. I don't like it because it means building on falsehood. Sometimes I say: 'If you cannot overcome it, make your decision.' "

Skorka then raised the issue that has caused such scandal in the Church, that of priestly sexual abuse of young people. Skorka said, "I would like to clarify that a priest who falls in love with a girl and then confesses is one thing, and a case of pedophilia is quite another. . . . Pedophilia has to be cut off at the roots. It's very serious. Two adults who love each other having an affair is something else."

Bergoglio responded:

> The idea that pedophilia is a consequence of celibacy is to be excluded. . . . More than 70 percent of cases of pedophilia occur in the family and local neighborhood: grandparents, uncles, stepfathers, neighbors. The problem is not one of celibacy. If a priest is a pedophile, he is so before he is a priest.
>
> Now, when that happens, we must never turn a blind eye. You cannot be in a position of power and destroy the life of another person. In the diocese it never happened to me, but a bishop once called me to ask me by phone what to do in situations like that and I told him to take away the priests' licenses, not to allow them to exercise the priesthood anymore,

and to begin a canonical trial in that diocese's court. I think that's the attitude to have. I do not believe in taking positions that uphold a certain corporative spirit in order to avoid damaging the image of the institution. That solution was proposed once in the United States: they proposed switching the priests to a different parish. It is a stupid idea; that way, the priest just takes the problem with him wherever he goes. The corporate reaction leads to such a result, so I do not agree with those solutions. Recently, there were cases uncovered in Ireland from about twenty years ago, and the present Pope [at the time, in 2010, Benedict XVI] clearly said: "Zero tolerance for that crime." I admire the courage and uprightness of Pope Benedict on the subject.

This conversation appears in the book *On Heaven and Earth (Sobre el cielo y la tierra)*, published in Spanish in Argentina in 2010 and in English by Image Books in the United States in 2013. It tells us something about how Pope Francis will face the continuing struggle to "purify" the Catholic Church: He will decisively follow the "zero tolerance" policy set in place by his predecessor.

CHAPTER 9

....

First Meeting with
President Kirchner

MARCH 18

Never in my life has a Pope kissed me!
—*President Cristina Kirchner of Argentina*

On Monday, March 18, Argentine president Cristina
Fernández de Kirchner came to Rome to visit the
archbishop who had become pope. And her visit shifted the
media spotlight toward Buenos Aires and Argentine issues.

One of the issues in their conversation, Mrs. Kirchner
said later, was the Falkland Islands, claimed by both Argentina and the United Kingdom, and evidently rich with as yet
untapped oil and gas fields. Kirchner told journalists she had
asked the pope to promote dialogue between the two sides.
Pope Francis, in the past, has said that the Falkland Islands,
though they are a United Kingdom overseas territory, belong
to Argentina.

"I asked for his intervention to avoid problems that could emerge from the militarization of Great Britain in the south Atlantic," Mrs. Kirchner told reporters after having lunch with the pope in the Domus Santa Marta. "We want a dialogue, and that's why we asked the Pope to intervene so that the dialogue is successful."

At a Mass last year, then Cardinal Bergoglio told Argentine veterans of the 1982 Falklands War: "We come to pray for all who have fallen, sons of the Homeland who went out to defend their mother, the Homeland, and to reclaim what is theirs." British prime minister David Cameron said when Bergoglio was elected pope that he "respectfully" disagreed with the view expressed in the past by Francis that the Falkland Islands had been "usurped" by the United Kingdom.

Mrs. Kirchner was the first head of state the new pope met. She presented him with a maté gourd and straw for drinking traditional Argentine tea. The two also kissed each other on the cheek, and Mrs. Kirchner remarked afterward: "Never in my life has a Pope kissed me!"

Despite the cordiality surrounding the meeting, relations between Pope Francis and President Kirchner have often been strained since 2004, soon after Néstor Kirchner, Mrs. Kirchner's predecessor and late husband, assumed the presidency.

During a speech on Wednesday night, just after the pope's election was announced, Mrs. Kirchner's young supporters whistled in protest when she mentioned the pope's name. They represent the left wing within Kirchnerism, and repudiate his alleged involvement in the human rights abuses of the Dirty War while serving as a high-ranking Jesuit. But there are others tensions as well between Pope Francis and sectors of Kirchner's political movement. Cardinal Bergoglio was a critic of Mr. Kirchner's rule and is believed to be aligned with the opposition in Argentina.

In 2009, Bergoglio criticized the level of poverty in the country, though the president had made efforts to curb poverty—such as heavy spending on social welfare. This is believed to have angered Mrs. Kirchner.

Now, with the wave of national pride and triumphalism following Pope Francis's election, Mrs. Kirchner may seek to renew ties to the Church as midterm elections loom in October 2013. "If relations remain broken with Pope Francis, it will be unpopular," says Leandro Bullor, an analyst at the University of Buenos Aires. "His words will influence society here and politicians will respond to that."

According to *El Jesuita* (The Jesuit), an authorized biography of Pope Francis by journalists Sergio Rubin and Francesca Ambrogetti published in 2010, Mr. Kirchner felt the Argentine Catholic Church "never recognized what he did to rescue the country from one of its worst crises," referring to Argentina's economic collapse of 2001. In 2005, Mr. Kirchner did not attend the *Te Deum*, an annual ceremony hosted by the archbishop of Buenos Aires to celebrate the anniversary of Argentina's first government in 1810. Soon after, Mr. Kirchner described Bergoglio as the "spiritual head of the political opposition."

"Bergoglio is close to Elisa Carrió, Gabriela Michetti, and Rabbi Sergio Bergman," Bullor has said. All three are fierce opponents of Kirchnerism.

New tensions have emerged in recent years. The Kirchners first pushed through legalization of same-sex marriage in 2010; then a gender identity law was passed in 2012 allowing people to change their sex without prior approval from a judge or doctor. A week before the same-sex marriage bill was passed, Bergoglio criticized it as an "attempt to confuse and trick God's children." Mrs. Kirchner branded his attitude "medieval." Still, despite this history, the lunch in the Domus Santa Marta by all accounts went well.

CHAPTER 10

························

Inaugural Mass

MARCH 19: FEAST OF ST. JOSEPH

You Are the Shepherd of the Sheep.
—*Motet composed by Pierluigi da Palestrina for the*
inauguration of a pontificate

On the Feast of St. Joseph, March 19, Pope Francis's pontificate officially began. "The correct term for the ceremony," Father Federico Lombardi of the Vatican Press Office clarified, "is not enthronement but inauguration. As successor of Peter, the pope is Bishop of Rome and the Church of Rome 'presides in love' over the others. Also, it is a celebration rich with symbols that recall the Pope's tie to St. Peter, beginning with the place where, according to tradition, Peter was martyred."

At about 8:45 A.M., Pope Francis left the Domus Santa Marta and started to greet the multitudes gathered in the various sections of the piazza. He went to the basilica's sacristy, via the Pietà side, at 9:15. Mass began at 9:30.

The pope, having entered the basilica, headed to St. Peter's tomb under the high altar, as trumpets played the *Tu es Petrus* (You are Peter). Francis venerated the tomb of St. Peter, together with the ten patriarchs and major archbishops of the Eastern Rite Catholic Churches (four of whom are cardinals). He then received the pallium, the ring, and a book of the Gospels that had been placed at St. Peter's tomb the night before.

The Holy Father then came back up from the Confession, as the tomb is called, to the main floor of the basilica, and the procession recommenced. The *Laudes Regiae* (Praises of the King) was chanted, with some invocations taken from the Vatican II document on the Church, *Lumen Gentium* (Light of the Nations). In the litany of saints, after the apostles, the holy Roman pontiffs most recently canonized up to the most recent, St. Pius X, were named.

The procession then exited the basilica.

On the left-hand side of the sagrato (porch of the basilica) were seated bishops and archbishops, about 250, as well as ecclesiastics and delegations from other churches and Christian confessions. On the right-hand side were delegations from various countries led by heads of state, ministers, and so on. On the St. Peter's statue side of the piazza were seated Jews, Muslims, and members of other religions, then around twelve hundred priests and seminarians. On the St. Paul's statue side were seated the diplomatic corps accredited to the Holy See and other civil authorities. The rest of the piazza was filled to capacity.

Concelebrating the Mass with Francis were all the cardinals present in Rome, joined by the patriarchs and major Eastern Rite archbishops (six); the secretary of the College of Cardinals; and two superior generals (that of the Order of Friars Minor, José Rodríguez Carballo, and that of the

Jesuits, Adolfo Nicolás Pachon, respectively president and vice president of the Union of Superior Generals). In total about 180 concelebrated.

The Imposition of the Pallium: Made of lamb's wool and sheep's wool, the pallium was placed on the pope's shoulders, recalling the Good Shepherd who carries the lost sheep on his shoulders. The pallium has five red crosses while the metropolitans' palliums have five black crosses. The one used by Francis was the same one that Benedict XVI used. It was placed on the pope's shoulders by Cardinal Proto-deacon Jean-Louis Tauran, and after the imposition, there was a prayer recited by Cardinal Proto-presbyter Godfried Danneels.

The Fisherman's Ring: Peter is the fisherman apostle, called to be a "fisher of men." The ring was presented to the pope by Cardinal Deacon Angelo Sodano (first of the Order of Bishops). Made of silver and gold, it bears the image of St. Peter with the keys and was designed by Enrico Manfrini. The ring was in the possession of Archbishop Pasquale Macchi, Pope Paul VI's personal secretary, and then Monsignor Ettore Malnati, who proposed it to Pope Francis through Cardinal Re.

The "Obedience": Six cardinals, two from each order, then approached the pope to make an act of obedience. (All the cardinal electors had already made an act of obedience in the Sistine Chapel at the end of the conclave and all the cardinals had been able to meet the pope in the following day's audience in the Clementine Hall.)

THE MASS was that of the Solemnity of St. Joseph, which has its own readings, not directly related to the rite of the inauguration of the pontificate.

The Gospel was read in Greek, showing the respect of the Latin Church for the Greek Churches (the Orthodox Churches). "Latin," Father Lombardi had said the previous day, "is already abundantly present in the other prayers and Mass parts."

The ceremony took about two hours. It would have been longer, but there was no offertory procession. The Eucharistic gifts were brought forward by the ministers who prepared the altar. Also, the pope did not distribute Communion, which was done by the deacons on the sagrato and, in the various areas of the piazza, by priests.

During the offertory the *Tu es pastor ovium* (You Are the Shepherd of the Sheep) motet composed by Pierluigi da Palestrina precisely for the inauguration of a pontificate was sung. At the conclusion, the *Te Deum* was sung with verses alternating between Gregorian chant and a melody by Tomás Luis de Victoria.

At the end of the celebration, and after removing the liturgical vestments, the pope went to the basilica's high altar to greet the heads of the official delegations from various countries. He then went to the Domus Santa Marta for lunch.

"The delegations," Father Lombardi emphasized, "are coming to Rome following information of the event made public by the Secretary of State. There were no 'invitations' sent out. All who wish to come are warmly welcomed. It must be made clear that no one has privileged status or will be refused. The order will depend on protocol and the level of the delegation."

The largest delegations were from Argentina, led by President Cristina Kirchner, and Italy, led by President Giorgio Napolitano and Prime Minister Mario Monti with presidents of the Italian Senate, House, and Constitutional Court.

The president of Taiwan, Ma Ying-jeou, along with his wife, also attended the Mass. At the end of the ceremony, Ma greeted the pope in Spanish, then, switching to English, mentioned an Argentine priest, Father Ricardo Ferreira, who had devoted fifty years of his life to serving Taiwan's people until he died of cancer in June 2006 at the age of eighty. Ma presented the pope with a gift of a porcelain vase decorated with two magpies. The vase echoed a mural from the 1700s in the Forbidden City in Beijing that was likely painted by apprentices of Giuseppe Castiglione, a Jesuit who had served as the emperor Qianlong's court painter at a time when the Catholic Church had an excellent relationship with China.

A Needed Message

During the Mass, the pope's homily drew on the work and image of St. Joseph, spouse of Mary, head of the Holy Family. The message was "to protect." This message is important at a time when the figure of the person who protects, be he a father, a mother, a priest, a scholar, a leader, is under profound attack—in a time when the protection is entrusted to others, or to no one, when the protectors are anonymous government officials, or hidden bureaucrats, or when they simply don't exist.

To protect means to make sure what one protects is not harmed, not hurt. And so this emphasis on protecting seemed to recall a passage in the Book of Revelation that focuses on "not hurting"; that is, protecting.

In chapter 7 of the Book of Revelation, an angel ascends "from the east," bearing "the seal of the living God." This angel cries out in a "loud voice" to the other "angels," who had been "hurting" the earth, and tells them to stop doing so. How does this passage relate to Pope Francis?

We know that St. Bonaventure (1221–1274) considered St. Francis (1181–1226) an appearance in history of this very angel, the "angel having the seal of the living God." He thought this because St. Francis had received the signs of Christ's wounds on his body (called the "stigmata") two years before his death, in 1224, after a fast of forty days on Mount Alverna in central Italy. St. Bonaventure writes about St. Francis in this way in his biography of Francis, the *Legenda Major* (approved by the Franciscan order in 1263).

We know also that Pope Emeritus Benedict XVI, in a talk on March 10, 2010, focused on St. Bonaventure's understanding of St. Francis's stigmata. Benedict on that occasion said that Bonaventure's "masterwork," the *Journey of the Mind into God*, a "manual" of mystical contemplation, was rooted in Bonaventure's meditation on St. Francis's stigmata. Bonaventure sought to understand how he, and we, might imitate St. Francis in drawing near to God, in being "sealed" by God.

"The last words of St. Bonaventure's *Itinerarium*, which responds to the question of how one can reach this mystical communion with God, would make one descend to the depth of the heart," Benedict said in 2010.

He cited St. Bonaventure: "If you now yearn to know how that happens (mystical communion with God), ask grace, not doctrine; desire, not the intellect; the groaning of prayer, not the study of the letter; the spouse, not the teacher; God, not man; darkness, not clarity; not light but the fire that inflames everything and transport to God with strong unctions and ardent affections. . . . We enter therefore into darkness, we silence worries, the passions and illusions; we pass with Christ Crucified from this world to the Father, so that, after having seen him, we say with Philip: that is enough for me" (*Itinerarium*, VII, 6).

Pope Emeritus Benedict on that occasion concluded: "Let us take up the invitation addressed to us by St. Bonaventure, the Seraphic Doctor, and let us enter the school of the divine Teacher: We listen to his Word of life and truth, which resounds in the depth of our soul. Let us purify our thoughts and actions, so that he can dwell in us, and we can hear his divine voice, which draws us toward true happiness."

Pope Francis was urging his listeners to be like St. Francis, to be like the "angel of the sixth seal" who was "sealed with the seal of the living God" and who told the other angels to cease "hurting" the earth.

Here is the relevant passage from the Book of Revelation: "And I saw another angel ascending from the east, having the seal of the living God: and he cried with a loud voice to the four angels, to whom it was given to hurt the earth and the sea, saying, 'Hurt not the earth, neither the sea, nor the trees, till we have sealed the servants of our God in their foreheads.'" (Rev 7:2–3)

So, as this pontificate begins under the sign of St. Joseph, the father, the protector, it also begins under the sign of St. Francis, the protector of the earth and of all who are on the earth, the man of peace.

Pope Francis is the pope of those who will protect, those who will defend others, those who will not "hurt the earth" or those who live on the earth.

Pope Francis's message could hardly have been more simple. Yet it expressed the essence of the Church's mission in the world: Every person matters. That is the root of all of Catholic social teaching, all Catholic moral teaching. Every person matters.

So simple, and yet, looking around at all the lonely people, all the hungry children, all the broken marriages, all those in despair, who can doubt that our world needs to hear this message?

CHAPTER 11

······························

First Meeting with Patriarch Bartholomew and with Metropolitan Hilarion

MARCH 20: LOOKING TO THE EAST

I also ask of you the kindness of a special prayer for myself, so that I might be a Pastor in harmony with Christ's heart.

—*Pope Francis, March 20, 2013, speaking to representatives of other Christian churches, and of other religions*

On the seventh day after his election Pope Francis greeted Patriarch Bartholomew, ecumenical patriarch of the Greek Orthodox Church. Based in Constantinople, "my brother Andrew," as the pope referred to him, had traveled to Rome to be present at Francis's inaugural Mass.

In the Gospels, Andrew was the brother of Simon Peter, the first bishop of Rome. They were fishermen together on the Sea of Galilee two thousand years ago. The patriarchs of Constantinople are considered the successors of the apostle

Andrew, and the popes of Rome are considered the successors of the apostle Peter.

So Pope Francis was saying that the friendship he feels toward the Orthodox reaches the level of fraternal feelings, that the two men, Francis and Bartholomew, are as the brothers Peter and Andrew.

Bartholomew's decision to travel to Rome for Pope Francis's installation "is an extraordinary event in the history of Christianity, and it is significant for reasons far beyond its novelty," writes George E. Demacopoulos, Ph.D., of the Orthodox Christian Studies Center, Fordham University, on the website of the Order of St. Andrew the Apostle.

The occasion is being presented in the media as something that has not happened since the ecclesiastical schism that separated Christian East and Christian West in the eleventh century. But that characterization is almost certainly wrong. This is quite likely the first time in history that a Bishop of Constantinople will attend the installation of a Bishop of Rome. And this is a profoundly bold step in ecumenical relations between the Orthodox and the Roman Catholics, one that could have lasting significance.

First and foremost, it is a powerful symbolic gesture for the cause of Christian unity. It demonstrates in unprecedented fashion the extent to which the Ecumenical Patriarch considers the relationship with the Roman Catholic Church to be a priority. For their part, members of the Vatican staff have responded to this grand gesture and have arranged for the reading of the Gospel at the installation to be sung in Greek (rather than Latin) in recognition of the fact that the

Ecumenical Patriarch has taken this unprecedented step.

The Christian world has been divided for so long that the establishment of an authentic reunion will require courage, leadership, and humility. It will also require a foundation in common faith and concerns. Given Pope Francis's well-documented work for social justice and his insistence that globalization is detrimental to the poor, it would appear as though the Orthodox and the Roman Catholic traditions have a renewed opportunity to work collectively on issues of mutual concern. With our Lord's assistance, that common cause can be transformed into more substantive theological work. But such work requires a first step and it would appear as though Ecumenical Patriarch Bartholomew is willing to take such a step.

Private Audiences

Just before the meeting with fraternal delegates, Pope Francis held a number of separate, smaller audiences. He received the following dignitaries:

- Her Excellency Dilma Vana Rousseff, president of Brazil, with an entourage
- His Holiness Bartholomew I, Greek Orthodox Ecumenical Patriarch of Constantinople
- Metropolitan Hilarion of Volokolamsk, of the Russian Orthodox Patriarchate of Moscow
- Claudio Epelman, executive director of the Latin American Jewish Congress

The Discourse to the Fraternal Delegates

Early on the afternoon of March 20, in the Clementine Hall of the Apostolic Palace, Pope Francis received fraternal delegates, that is, representative envoys of churches, ecclesial communities, and international ecumenical organizations, as well as representatives of non-Christian religions, who had come to Rome for his inauguration.

On behalf of those present, the Ecumenical Patriarch of Constantinople, Bartholomew I, greeted the pope, recalling the "elevated, serious, and difficult task" that his ministry bears. He reiterated the need for the churches to shun worldly distractions and to work on the unity between Christians.

Francis, who listened to the words of the patriarch seated on an armchair rather than the throne that is customarily used in the Clementine Hall, thanked Bartholomew. He then said that, thanks to the presence at yesterday's Mass of representatives of the various communities, he had felt "in an even stronger way, the prayer for unity among the believers in Christ" and he had glimpsed, in their presence, its eventual "full realization, which depends on God's plan and our sincere cooperation.

"I begin my apostolic ministry," he continued, "in this year that my venerated predecessor, Pope Benedict XVI, with a truly inspired intuition, proclaimed the Year of Faith for the Catholic Church. With this initiative, which I wish to continue and which I hope serves as a stimulus for each of us in our journey of faith, he wanted to commemorate the fiftieth anniversary of the Second Vatican Council, proposing a type of pilgrimage to what is essential for every Christian:

a personal and transforming relationship with Jesus Christ, the Son of God, who died and rose again for our salvation. The heart of the Council's message lies precisely in the desire to proclaim this ever-valid treasure of the faith to the persons of our time."

So, once again, this new pope was speaking of the need for a personal relationship with the resurrected and living Lord, Jesus Christ. He was not speaking about "studying" the faith, or "studying" the life and works of Jesus, he was speaking about a "relationship" with Jesus.

Francis then spoke about the need for Christian unity. He recalled the image and words of Pope John XXIII at the opening of the Second Vatican Council:

> The Catholic Church considers it her duty to actively work so as to bring about the great mystery of that unity for which Jesus Christ prayed so ardently to His Father in heaven on the eve of his sacrifice. . . .
> Yes, dear brothers and sisters in Christ, we all feel intimately joined in our Saviour's prayer at the Last Supper, to his call: *"ut unum sint."* Let us call on our merciful Father that we may fully live that faith that we received as a gift on the day of our Baptism and to be able to witness to it freely, joyfully, and courageously. This will be the best way we can serve the cause of unity among Christians, a service of hope for a world that is still marked by divisions, differences, and rivalries.
> For my part, I wish to assure you, following in the path of my predecessors, of my firm will to continue

on the path of ecumenical dialogue.... I ask you
to take my cordial greetings and assurance of my
remembrance in the Lord Jesus to the Churches and
Christian Communities that you represent here. I
also ask of you the kindness of a special prayer for
myself, so that I might be a Pastor in harmony with
Christ's heart.

Then, addressing the representatives of the Jewish communities, he emphasized "the very special spiritual bond"
that they have with Christians.

Quoting the very important, and sometimes neglected,
Vatican II declaration *Nostra Aetate* (1965), he said: "'The
Church of Christ acknowledges that ... the beginnings of
her faith and her election are found already among the Patriarchs, Moses and the prophets.' ... I am confident that, with
the help of the Almighty, we can profitably continue that
fraternal dialogue that the Council hoped for and that has
been carried out, bearing not a few fruits, especially over the
last few decades."

The pope then greeted those belonging to other religious
traditions, first of all the Muslims, who "adore the one, living, and merciful God and who call upon Him in prayer."
This outreach was to elicit some criticism from opponents
of Islam in the West, but the words of Francis were quite
clear: He wishes to engage the Muslims in dialogue, as respected partners.

So this was also a programmatic meeting, in which the
pope laid out a broad-ranging program of discussion, dialogue, and friendship with other Christians, with Jews, with
Muslims, and with others of goodwill.

Metropolitan Hilarion Meets
Again with Pope Francis

Also on March 20, Pope Francis of Rome met with Metropolitan Hilarion of Volokolamsk, chairman of the Moscow Patriarchate's Department for External Church Relations and a high-level representative of Patriarch Kirill, the head of the Russian Orthodox Church. The meeting took place at the Vatican Secretariat of State. This meeting was significant because Russia is an important country—the center of the Soviet Union for seventy years, and still one sixth of the landmass of the earth, filled with natural resources like oil, gas, minerals, and timber—and because the Russian Orthodox Church, which has been reemerging since 1991, after persecution under Communism, is the most numerous of the fourteen national Orthodox Churches.

At the beginning of the meeting, Hilarion conveyed to Pope Francis warm greetings and gratitude for prayers from His Holiness Patriarch Kirill of Moscow and All Russia and noted that the primate of the Russian Orthodox Church had closely followed the process of election and enthronement. Metropolitan Hilarion presented the pope with Patriarch Kirill's book *Freedom and Responsibility* in the Spanish language. Pope Francis conveyed his sincere best wishes to the primate of the Russian Orthodox Church.

Hilarion told Pope Francis about the life and ministry of the Russian Orthodox Church and expressed his hope that the good strides in the development of relations between the Russian Orthodox Church and the Roman Catholic Church, made during the pontificate of Benedict XVI, would be ensured. Hilarion added that the Moscow Patriarchate attached great importance to the development of relations with the Catholic Church, particularly in the field of social ministry, aid to the poor and the destitute, and protection of the persecuted.

Hilarion also told the pope about the problems still existing between the two Churches, and expressed his hope for finding ways to their solution during the new pontificate.

At the end of the meeting, Hilarion handed a gift from Patriarch Kirill, an icon of the Mother of God, called *Look Down with Favour on My Lowliness*, to Pope Francis, noting that "the first steps of Your Holiness after the election were marked by lowliness and humility."

Pope Francis replied that he lacked humility and asked for prayers to the Lord to grant it to him.

The talk was held in the Russian and Spanish languages and was translated by Miguel Palacio, one of Hilarion's assistants.

One Lung to Make Two Lungs

The new pope has many daunting challenges ahead, and one of the greatest is to overcome the thousand-year division between Catholics and the Orthodox, which dates to the year A.D. 1054, when the pope of Rome and the patriarch of Constantinople mutually excommunicated each other. That break launched what has come to be known as the Great Schism—between East and West, the Greek and the Latin worlds, the Orthodox and the Roman Catholics. It has been a desire of the last few popes, and not a few Orthodox, to overcome this division, to reunite the two branches of Christianity, and in so doing, to make Western culture, European cultures, "breathe with two lungs," in the expression of Pope John Paul II, who strongly favored this process.

Francis will have to try to make Europe "breathe with two lungs," and he will have to do it with just one lung himself. The Argentine pontiff lost the greater part of one lung to an infection when he was about the age of twenty. "He feels it today," his authorized biographer, Sergio Rubin, has said. "He's a little bit slowed by it, but he's okay."

Doctors said that losing one lung did not necessarily compromise the pope's health or reduce his life span, though it means no strenuous exercise, since he no longer has as much air capacity. "He probably wouldn't be able to run marathons, but I don't think that would be on his schedule," Dr. Peter Openshaw, director of the Centre for Respiratory Infection at Imperial College London, told a reporter. "Having one lung should be enough as long as there is no other disease in that lung."

Openshaw did not think a papal schedule would be too taxing for Francis's one lung, though he noted the pope's rib cage might look slightly unusual. "His x-ray will probably look rather alarming, but understandable once you know he only has one lung," he said.

Openshaw said Francis's existing lung would probably have expanded to fill the space left by the missing one, and that his rib cage would have shrunk slightly. His diaphragm may also have moved up slightly higher than normal.

Experts said it would be rare nowadays to remove a lung. Antibiotics would be used to treat most lung infections including tuberculosis, though part of the organ might be removed to treat advanced lung cancer. But when Francis had his lung removed, the available antibiotics were not as powerful. "In the past, doctors used all kinds of strange things to try to treat lung infections," Dr. Jennifer Quint, a respiratory expert at London's School of Hygiene and Tropical Medicine, told a journalist. She said physicians even used to stick Ping-Pong balls into people's lungs in an attempt to starve the lungs of oxygen, to kill the bacteria.

Quint said the fact that Francis appears so fit and healthy at seventy-six bodes well for his future. "If he were going to have any major complications from the surgery [to remove the lung], he would have had them by now." She said Francis's main challenge would be to keep his remaining lung healthy. "I would recommend a yearly flu vaccination and an occasional pneumonia vaccine to avoid infection," she said.

Openshaw agreed the pope's remaining lung should be able to compensate for the missing one, similar to how parts of the brain may pick up functions of other regions damaged by a stroke. "The other lung can gain capacity, but there will be limits," he said, comparing it to a car engine that now runs slightly more slowly. "You may not be able to accelerate as hard but it still works just as well."

"Pope Francis Did Not Denounce Me"

Also on March 20, Father Francisco Jalics, who was imprisoned by the Argentine regime for five months in the 1970s, issued a statement saying that he and the new pope had "reconciled" in the year 2000. It had been alleged in the press that Jalics blamed Pope Francis, who during the 1970s was a Jesuit regional superior in Argentina, for his arrest, at least in part. And this had led to many reports that Father Bergoglio had in some way been an "accomplice" of the military regime of that decade.

Bergoglio's association with the dictatorship was related to the testimony of María Elena Funes, a catechist who was detained by authorities following the arrest and subsequent disappearance of two Jesuit priests.

"I myself was once inclined to believe that we were the victims of a denunciation," Jalics said in his online statement. "[But] at the end of the 1990s, after numerous conversations, it became clear to me that this suspicion was unfounded. It is therefore wrong to assert that our capture took place at the initiative of Father Bergoglio."

In a comment made just after Pope Francis's election, Jalics had said that he and Bergoglio had reconciled and "hugged solemnly" in 2000. But in that statement he had been noncommittal, saying he "could not comment on the role played by Father Bergoglio in these events." Argentine critics of the pope had therefore continued to accuse him of wrongdoing, based on documents and old testimonies of Yorio, who died several years ago. Jalics's failure to deny these accusations added to their suspicions.

But in his new statement, Jalics was categorical: "Some commentaries imply the opposite of what I meant," he said. "The fact is: Orlando Yorio and I were not denounced by Father Bergoglio."

Vatican spokesman Father Federico Lombardi had said on March 15, two days after the new pope's election, that, on the contrary, "there have been many declarations demonstrating how much Bergoglio did to protect many persons at the time."

And this was corroborated by Argentine Nobel Peace Prize winner Adolfo Pérez Esquivel. Bergoglio "had no links with the dictatorship" that ruled Argentina between 1976 and 1983, Pérez Esquivel told BBC News on March 14. "There were bishops who were accomplices of the dictatorship, but it was not the case of Bergoglio. Bergoglio was questioned because it is said he did not do enough to get out of jail two priests, as he was the Superior of the Jesuits. But I know personally that many bishops called on the military junta for the release of prisoners and priests and these requests were not granted," said Pérez Esquivel.

Pope Francis received support also in the days after his election from an unlikely source: Viggo Mortensen, the actor who played Aragorn in the film version of J. R. R. Tolkien's classic, profoundly Christian trilogy, *The Lord of the Rings*.

In an interview by Andrew O'Hehir for Salon.com after the pope's election, titled "Viggo Mortensen: Lay Off the Pope: *The Lord of the Rings* star, who shares a soccer team with the pope, has known him for years and defends his honor," Mortensen reveals that he and the pope are fans of the same soccer team in Buenos Aires.

"He's been a fan since he was a little kid. He grew up with that team, he did a lot of his work as a Jesuit priest in that neighborhood, which is a pretty poor neighborhood. There's a lot of problems in that neighborhood: poverty, drugs, crime. He comes from that Jesuit tradition of helping the needy."

Asked if he personally knew anything about Bergoglio, Mortensen replied: "Yeah, I know about him a lot. . . . I know initially when he was named there were a lot of rumors circulated about his complicity with the dictatorial regime in the '70s, and that was disproved. . . . There's a lot of malicious gossip, and I suppose it's not just a left-wing thing, or right-wing thing. It might be people who don't think much of the Catholic Church, people who have grudges. . . .

"People who knew him well—human rights activists, including the Nobel Peace Prize winner in 1980, and also a

woman judge who in 1973 was kicked out of the country—
people who have been treated really badly and, if it was true,
would have every reason to speak against him—have come
out staunchly defending him. . . . The Church is definitely
guilty of a lot of things during that period, but I don't see
that he was, frankly."

CHAPTER 12

....

Diplomats: Holding to Benedict

MARCH 22

> But there is another form of poverty! It is the spiritual poverty of our time, which afflicts the so-called richer countries particularly seriously. It is what my much-loved predecessor, the dear and venerated Benedict XVI, called the "tyranny of relativism."
>
> —*Pope Francis, citing words spoken by Pope Benedict XVI*
> *on the eve of the 2005 conclave*

On the ninth day after his election, and on the third day after he was officially installed as pope, March 22, Francis spoke to the Vatican diplomatic corps, representing 160 nations with whom the Holy See has diplomatic relations, in the Sala Regia in the Vatican.

In his address to the diplomats, Pope Francis took his stand with his predecessor.

The importance of Francis's words cannot be overestimated. The new pope, despite reports that he was very "different" and represented a "new direction" and a "new vision" for the Church, made clear that he shared the central essential spiritual vision of Pope Benedict. And in this talk, unlike in several previous talks, Pope Francis adhered strictly to his prepared text; he made no off-the-cuff remarks. So, his words were meditated and intentional.

If one were to summarize in a single sentence what he said to the diplomats, it could be this: "I stand with Pope Benedict." But stand with Pope Benedict on what, precisely? What Francis said was critical, and should be read carefully by all seeking to understand where the new pope is coming from.

In the first days after his election, many observers "circled" Pope Francis, like those blind men who circled the elephant in the well-known fable, trying to understand what it was without being able to see it. One touched the rope-like tail, and said the elephant was a python; one touched the smooth, sheet-like ear, and said the elephant was flat and thin; one touched the hard, ivory tusk, and said the elephant was a dangerous creature with no features except a sharp point. Each "saw" only a small part; none saw the whole.

And so one observer noted the pope's simplicity, his actual poverty, his love for the poor, and said (wrongly): "He is the people's pope, the pope of the poor, so . . . he is a liberal, he may very well be a social revolutionary, a 'liberation' pope . . . and perhaps also break with 'conservative' Church teaching on sexual matters."

Another pundit noted that Francis had strongly defended Church teaching on the family, on traditional Christian sexual morality, and said (wrongly): "He is a conservative, he won't 'rock the boat' at all."

Neither vision is sufficient; neither is accurate. Francis can in no way be "captured" by these simplistic, irrelevant, political "categories." He transcends them. Precisely as Jesus himself transcended all categories, reaching out to sinners— and all are sinners—but also asking them not to sin. Loving the sinner, but not the sin. Precisely as Pope Benedict cease-lessly reminded all of us that our destiny as human beings transcends all worldly categories, that we are made for eter-nity, not just for time.

Perhaps it is time we realize that there are not "con-servative" and "liberal," or even "traditional" and "ortho-dox," Catholics at all. We are only Catholics in a universal Church, stretching back to the first days of the Church and forward to the end of the world in time, and global in space.

In any case, Pope Francis, speaking to the diplomats, powerfully set his course, transcending the "left" and the "right," and pointing all of us toward higher things. It was the first great programmatic discourse of his pontificate.

His central thrust was: (1) don't try to confine me, or re-duce me and my message to worldly categories; and (2) don't try to separate me from my predecessor, Benedict. The sig-nature phrase was that there is "spiritual poverty" as well as "physical" poverty—a central message of Christianity, and a central message of Pope Benedict.

Pope Francis said there is truth accessible to human be-ings, a truth that gives life and light, a truth that relativism, in its denial that any truth can be absolute, obscures, leav-ing confusion, darkness, and ultimately, death (as Pope John Paul II put it, helping to create a "culture of death").

He developed this argument beginning with a reference to the reasons that he chose the name Francis.

The new pope said: "As you know, there are various rea-sons why I chose the name of Francis of Assisi. . . . One of the first reasons was Francis's love for the poor. How many poor people there still are in the world! And what great suffering they have to endure!" Then he added: "But there is another form of poverty! It is the spiritual poverty of our time, which afflicts the so-called richer countries particularly seriously. It is what my much-loved predecessor, Benedict XVI, called the 'tyranny of relativism,' which makes everyone his own criterion and endangers the coexistence of peoples."

So Francis was making his own the thought of Pope Emeritus Benedict on a key problem with modern secular society, the problem of a moral relativism that argues that all truth is relative and no human action can be definitively labeled as "good" or "evil."

Eight years ago, on April 18, 2005, this same thought was at the heart of then cardinal Joseph Ratzinger's homily to the cardinals as they were about to go into the conclave that elected him. Here are those historic passages:

> How many winds of doctrine have we known in recent decades, how many ideological currents, how many ways of thinking. The small boat of the thought of many Christians has often been tossed about by these waves—flung from one extreme to another: from Marxism to liberalism, even to libertinism; from collectivism to radical individualism; from atheism to a vague religious mysticism; from agnosticism to syncretism, and so forth. Every day new sects spring up, and what St. Paul says about human deception and the trickery that strives to entice people into error (cf. Eph 4:14) comes true.
>
> Today, having a clear faith based on the Creed of the Church is often labeled as fundamentalism. Whereas relativism, that is, letting oneself be "tossed here and

there, carried about by every wind of doctrine," seems the only attitude that can cope with modern times. We are building a *dictatorship of relativism* that does not recognize anything as definitive and whose ultimate goal consists solely of one's own ego and desires.

We, however, have a different goal: the Son of God, the true man. He is the measure of true humanism. An "adult" faith is not a faith that follows the trends of fashion and the latest novelty; a mature adult faith is deeply rooted in friendship with Christ. It is this friendship that opens us up to all that is good and gives us a criterion by which to distinguish the true from the false, and deceit from truth.

We must develop this adult faith; we must guide the flock of Christ to this faith. And it is this faith—only faith—that creates unity and is fulfilled in love.

By using this same phrase, "dictatorship of relativism," Pope Francis was linking his own thought, and faith, and the direction of his pontificate, to these words of then cardinal Joseph Ratzinger.

Some other points are very important in Pope Francis's discourse:

- The new pope's desire to engage in dialogue with Islam, something he expressed in very clear terms, is something many Western powers, which since September 11, 2001, have entered into a seemingly endless conflict with large parts of the Islamic world, will certainly note with interest.
- The new pope is concerned for creation, that human beings take care not to "hurt the earth."

- Pope Francis expresses a clear desire that "those few countries that do not yet have diplomatic relations with the Holy See"—like China—may soon establish relations.

Pope Francis did not deliver this address in French—the language traditionally used by popes in such diplomatic settings. It is said that Pope Francis both understands and speaks French—and a bit of English as well—but has been reluctant to use those languages in public, preferring to speak in Italian, which he speaks fluently. This explains why, except for a few lines spoken in Spanish, all his public speaking during his first days as pope has been in Italian.

White Chair, Not a Throne

Concerning small details, Pope Francis had already made a number of changes during his first days as pope. His open attitude was obvious.

During his first nine days, he used the traditional throne seat only once. In all his other meetings, with religious leaders and diplomats, Pope Francis has used a simple white chair, which is usually reserved for weekly general audiences. Also, the chair was not elevated on a platform but rather kept on the same level as other seats. In fact, during his meeting with religious leaders, the new pope used the same type of chair used by the guests.

Further Comments on the New Pope

Also on March 22, a number of comments on the new pope's election gave deeper insight into the man and his spiritual vision. Through these comments, published by the television news agency Rome Reports, we learned that the person who was the most surprised by the election of Cardinal Jorge Bergoglio was the Argentine cardinal himself.

The auxiliary bishop of Buenos Aires, who had lived with the pope for the past ten years, explained how the election changed the new pope's original plans. "His future plans were, once his resignation was accepted and his successor named, to live at a home in Buenos Aires for elderly and sick priests," Monsignor Eduardo Garcia said. "He had already picked his room. He also would have led a life of prayer, as an adviser to many, of spirituality, of celebrating Mass at the parishes. A normal life without governance."

After many years of working with him on a daily basis, Monsignor Garcia said the pope's style is natural, and coincides well with his need to interact and be close to people.

"No one calls in his name," Garcia said. "When he was to give an interview, he has to give the answer, he has to say something. No one else will do it for him. He will call you directly to tell you to come tomorrow at this time. With this he is very independent in his desire for direct communication."

During his years at the helm of the Church in Buenos Aires, then cardinal Jorge Bergoglio's teachings and writings had established clear guidelines. "There are three words that can define him: unity, truth, and mercy," Garcia said. "Those are the words." The auxiliary bishop of Buenos Aires said Pope Francis's unpredictability, deep down, is natural, an extension of his faith, even though some perceive it as odd. "These are his anomalies," he said. "They may seem like anomalies, but we've been deforming life, and what should be normal, now seems odd. It's to be beside those who need us, or to go beyond preestablished notions to speak to one another; it may seem odd, but it's not."

The archbishop of Budapest, Cardinal Peter Erdö, sixty, among the youngest cardinal electors, took part in the March 13 conclave and also was present in the 2005 conclave. He told Rome Reports that the fact that Bergoglio chose the name Francis was very telling of his style and spirituality.

Erdö said, "I think he wants to give a new push to the spiritual life of the Church. Back in his time, St. Francis of Assisi represented a type of novelty, not only socially but at a spiritual level."

Erdö also talked about how the new pope was the chancellor of the Pontifical Catholic University of Argentina, so he believes the importance of education will be a pillar of the new pontificate. "He wants to be able to transmit the faith in a simple, direct way to everyday people," Erdö said. "But he also wants to show the richness of faith through a scientific, high-level conversation."

So Pope Francis will likely use the papacy to continue this work in a more global way. He will undoubtedly support Catholic education, dialogue between faith and science, and assist the poor through support of better education for children and young people. All of this will be a concentrated effort to help those around the world to develop not only intellectually, but spiritually as well.

CHAPTER 13

....

First Meeting with
Pope Emeritus Benedict

MARCH 23: "WE ARE BROTHERS"

Very beautiful.

—*Father Federico Lombardi, S.J., on the first embrace between*
Pope Francis and Pope Emeritus Benedict XVI at Castel Gandolfo

Francis Meets Benedict

The following is based on a Vatican Radio report on the first meeting between the new pope, Francis, and the former pope, Benedict XVI.

While it had been expected that Pope Emeritus Benedict would meet Pope Francis in the palace itself, Benedict came to the helicopter landing pad about a mile from the palace, to greet Francis.

The two men met alone for forty-five minutes before having lunch, where they were joined by their secretaries.

Speaking exclusively to Vatican Radio, the director of the Holy See Press Office, Father Federico Lombardi, S.J., revealed the details of the historic encounter, which he described as a moment of "profound and elevated communion":

The helicopter landed in Castel Gandolfo heliport, at about 12:15, and the car with the retired Pope approached the helicopter landing site.

The Holy Father alighted: he was accompanied by the Substitute [Secretary of State] Msgr. Becciu, by Msgr. Leonardo Sapienza, and Msgr. Alfred Xuereb.

As the Pope alighted, the Pope Emeritus approached him and there was a moving embrace between the two.

Then there followed brief greetings with those others present—the Bishop of Albano and the Director of the Pontifical Villas, Mr. Petrillo—they all got in the car: Pope Francis on the right, the place reserved to the Pope, and the Pope Emeritus on the left. Msgr. Georg Gänswein, who is Prefect of the Papal Household, traveled in the same car. And so the car brought the two protagonists of this historic meeting to the elevators and they went up to the apartments and immediately went to the chapel for a moment of prayer.

In the chapel, the Pope Emeritus offered the place of honor to Pope Francis, but he said: "We are brothers," and wanted them to kneel together in the same pew.

After a short moment of prayer, they then went to the private library where, at about 12:30, the private meeting began. This is the library where the Pope normally receives important guests in Castel Gandolfo.

Pope Francis brought a beautiful icon as a gift for the Pope Emeritus. It was an icon of Our Lady of

Humility, as a gift for Benedict XVI's great humility. Their discussions ended at 13:15, lasting about forty-five minutes.

It should be noted, with regard to the clothing, . . . the Pope Emeritus wears a simple cassock, white, without a sash and without a mantella: these are the two details which distinguish his clothing from that of Pope Francis, who wears a mantella and sash.

The two secretaries, Msgr. Georg Gänswein and Msgr. Alfred Xuereb, are expected to eat lunch with them. Thus the totally private and confidential meeting ended with the discussions in the library.

The Pope Emeritus will also accompany Pope Francis to the heliport, when the time comes for his return.

Let us remember that this is not their first meeting: it is their first face-to-face meeting, but Pope Francis had many times already addressed his thoughts to the Pope Emeritus, during his first appearance on the central Loggia, and then two personal calls: the night of his election and St. Joseph's Day.

Thus, the dialogue had already started, even though the personal, physical meeting had not yet taken place.

Let us also remember that the retired Pope had already expressed his unconditional reverence and obedience to his successor at his farewell meeting with the Cardinals, February 28, and certainly in this [today's] meeting—which was a moment of profound and elevated communion—will have had the opportunity to renew this act of reverence and obedience to his successor, and certainly Pope Francis renewed his gratitude and that of the whole Church for Pope Benedict's ministry during his pontificate.

Father Lombardi excluded the possibility of Pope Francis and Benedict XVI appearing at the balcony together to greet the public.

The Icon of Mary

The words that remain from the first meeting of the present and former popes are the ones spoken by Pope Francis to Benedict: "We are brothers."

As Nicole Winfield put it in her comprehensive Associated Press dispatch: "The two men in white embraced and showed one another the deference owed a Pope in ways that surely turned Vatican protocol upside down: A reigning Pope telling a retired one, 'We are brothers,' and insisting that they pray side by side during a date to discuss the future of the Catholic Church."

In the same report, she noted: "Francis also brought a gift for Benedict, an icon of the Madonna. 'They told me it's the Madonna of Humility,' Francis told Benedict. 'Let me say one thing: When they told me that, I immediately thought of you, at the many marvelous examples of humility and gentleness that you gave us during your pontificate.' Benedict replied: '*Grazie, grazie.*'"

The icon Pope Francis gave to Pope Emeritus Benedict was the very icon Russian Orthodox metropolitan Hilarion had given to Francis three days before. I asked Hilarion how he felt about Pope Francis's decision. "Very pleased and touched," he responded.

Now, what does all this mean? At the first meeting ever of the two popes of the Roman Catholic Church, there was a Russian connection and an Orthodox connection joining them: an image of the Virgin Mary, the Madonna of Humility, brought from Russia.

To me, it also suggests that Mary, Mother of the Church, is watching over the Church in these difficult and dangerous times, and acting as a mother even to these two men, Benedict and Francis, bringing them together.

I sense in this a mysterious design, a mystical design, for the Christian Church to return to greater unity, East and West, Greek and Latin, Orthodox and Catholic—with one of the great hinge points being Russia.

The Madonna of Humility . . . It is precisely humility that brings these two popes together. One dedicated to a life of thought, to theology; the other dedicated to a life of action, to pastoral care of the poor. But both very simple and humble. And the way to proceed toward greater Christian unity is this same way, the way of Mary, the way of humility.

It brings to mind the conclusion of the homily at the Mass for his installation, when Pope Francis asked specifically for Mary's intercession:

> To protect Jesus with Mary, to protect the whole
> of creation, to protect each person, especially the
> poorest, to protect ourselves: this is a service that
> the Bishop of Rome is called to carry out, yet one
> to which all of us are called, so that the star of hope
> will shine brightly. Let us protect with love all that
> God has given us!
>
> I implore the intercession of the Virgin Mary,
> Saint Joseph, Saints Peter and Paul, and Saint
> Francis, that the Holy Spirit may accompany my
> ministry, and I ask all of you to pray for me! Amen.

Don Georg

Francis has not been entirely alone during his first days as pope. Observers have noted a discreet presence on a number of occasions: Archbishop Georg Gänswein, the personal secretary of Pope Emeritus Benedict XVI and the Prefect of the Pontifical Household. Gänswein is the "connection" between the pope emeritus and Pope Francis. He was at Francis's side during many of his first public appearances: during his visit to St. Mary Major to pray and when he paid his bill at the desk of the Vatican priest's residence, at the meeting with all the cardinals of the Church the next day, and at the meeting with journalists in the Paul VI Audience Hall on the third day. "The role of Archbishop Gänswein at the beginning of this pontificate goes beyond that of Prefect of the Pontifical Household," wrote Giacomo Galeazzi, an Italian Vaticanist, in *VaticanInsider* on March 17. "An entirely new figure in ecclesiastical history, Georg is the point of contact between the reigning Pope and the Emeritus one. He preserves his function as Ratzinger's Secretary and continues to live with him at Castel Gandolfo, but at the same time he runs the Pontificalis Domus of his successor Bergoglio. Beyond any protocol, he substantially acts as a transmission belt in the difficult starting phase of the pontificate."

It is not known how Pope Francis and Gänswein relate to each other, but Galeazzi wrote that Gänswein "really likes this pontiff, who is so different from 'his.'"

The existence of this triangular relationship between Pope Francis, Gänswein, and Pope Emeritus Benedict means that there can be continuity between the two pontificates. As Pope Francis begins to confront issues like the Vatileaks scandal, the return of the Lefebvrists to communion with

Rome, the reform of the Curia, and the Vatican bank, he will have Gänswein near him, and Gänswein will also be near Pope Emeritus Benedict.

"He is performing a very delicate task," a Vatican official told Galeazzi, referring to Gänswein. Gänswein "has the Vatileaks dossier to be delivered to Francis," the official said, referring to the report by the three cardinals who, at the request of then pope Benedict, spent nearly a year investigating the circumstances of the Vatileaks affair: Julian Herranz, Jozef Tomko, and Salvatore De Giorgi.

As the first days of the new pontificate unfolded, and Pope Francis continued to live in the Domus Santa Marta, he also became closer to Don Battista Ricca, the director of the Domus, who was said to join Pope Francis for many of his meals. Also, the "second secretary" of then pope Benedict, a monsignor from Malta named Alfred Xuereb, fifty-four, has emerged as the acting personal secretary of Pope Francis.

CHAPTER 14

······················

Palm Sunday Mass

MARCH 24

Prepare well—prepare spiritually above all—in your communities, so that our gathering in Rio may be a sign of faith for the whole world.

—*Pope Francis, Palm Sunday Mass, March 24, 2013,*
in St. Peter's Square, homily to young people planning
to go to World Youth Day in Brazil

The Unique King: Joy, Cross, Youth

Pope Francis, eleven days after his election, celebrated the joyous first Palm Sunday Mass of his pontificate.

He used the occasion to emphasize in his homily the contrast between the joy of Jesus' wonderful entry in Jerusalem—"praise, blessing, peace: joy fills the air"—and the suffering that awaits Jesus in just a few short days—"Jesus enters Jerusalem to die on the Cross."

But, as on several other occasions in the first days of his

pontificate, he also referred to the devil, saying: "We must not believe the Evil One when he tells us: you can do nothing to counter violence, corruption, injustice, your sins! We must never grow accustomed to evil! With Christ we can transform ourselves and the world."

His references to the devil, to the Evil One, as a reality (that is, actor, agent, and so, evidently, a personal being) in our world have struck many across the spectrum of Catholic and secular thought.

It will take time to grasp the true meaning of this pope's teaching on this subject, but we can take a first stab at analysis. Clearly Francis is saying there is something, or someone, "out there" that deceives, harms, must be fought against. There is a real battle; not everything, or everyone, is good; choices must be made, difficult ones, to overcome "violence, corruption, injustice" and, not least, to overcome "your sins."

In this sense, the essence of the pope's preaching is to return to reality. Christian realism. Far from "pie in the sky" Christian avoidance of tough struggles for earthly social justice, but also, and importantly, personal sanctity.

Francis's actions have shown us that he wishes to live simply, humbly, with the poor. And his teaching is now echoing that: that we must work, and struggle, and be committed, first to Christ, then to our brothers and sisters, and in this way, with great realism, to "incarnate" our faith.

And it is in this sense that he turned to the topic of World Youth Day, which is planned for July in Rio de Janeiro. He confirmed that he will go to Brazil (God willing), and he asked the young people to "prepare themselves," saying: "Prepare well—prepare spiritually above all—in your communities, so that our gathering in Rio may be a sign of faith for the whole world."

Again, "prepare well" means to take the journey seriously, gathering what one needs, but in this case, the preparations are of faith. We can imagine that more specific recommendations may soon be given.

After celebrating the Mass, Pope Francis made his way through St. Peter's Square in an open popemobile. He stopped many times, blessing and kissing babies and toddlers. Once, the pope got out of the vehicle to greet a group of people. He also blessed many pilgrims with physical disabilities. In those minutes, he seemed to share the joy that Jesus himself may have felt entering Jerusalem.

For the new pope, it was a happy, peaceful day, filled with the praise and love of thousands, and under a serene blue sky.

Will Francis Travel to Jerusalem?

> I've invited Pope Francis to the Holy Land. —*Latin Rite patriarch Fouad Twal of Jerusalem, speaking on March 22 to the Aid to the Church in Need news service*

The Latin patriarch of Jerusalem, Fouad Twal, has invited Pope Francis to visit the Holy Land, according to Oliver Maksan, of ACN news service's Jerusalem bureau.

At the same time, he spoke about how he knew the new pope:

> I met Pope Francis when he was still the Cardinal Archbishop of Buenos Aires. That was on the occasion of my visit to the Palestinian diaspora in Argentina

about two years ago. Cardinal Bergoglio, as he then
was, knew the situation of the Palestinians in Argentina and other Latin American countries very well.

At that time I gave a talk in his presence in which
I called for a just peace in the Middle East and for
mutual respect and tolerance between the different peoples there. Cardinal Bergoglio expressed his
agreement.

But independently of this he will, I am sure, love
the Holy Land as all popes have done and will be concerned about us here.

Twal continued that this hope was also justified in the
light of the Holy Father's reputation as the pope of the poor:
"Here in the Middle East, and especially in Syria, there are
many people who live in poverty and are suffering."

In addition to the Latin patriarch, both the Israeli president, Shimon Peres, and the president of the autonomous
Palestinian National Authority, Mahmoud Abbas, have
invited the Holy Father to visit the Holy Land. Peres said
that the new pope was a welcome guest. He could help bring
peace to a turbulent area. Abbas has invited the pope to visit
Christ's place of birth in Bethlehem. In his letter of con-
gratulation on the election, he expressed his wish that Pope
Francis would commit himself to the cause of peace in the
Holy Land.

In the meantime, the media are reporting that Pope
Francis intends to visit Jerusalem in the coming year together with the ecumenical patriarch Bartholomew I. The
Church leaders thus intended to recall the historic meeting
between Pope Paul VI and the then ecumenical patriarch

Athenagoras in the Holy City fifty years ago. The Vatican has not yet confirmed this information.

Rosa Margherita, Francis's "Theologian" Grandmother

As he usually does, Francis added a few off-the-cuff words during his Palm Sunday homily.

After reading the phrases "wounds inflicted upon humanity" and "greed for money," he looked up and said: "Our grandmother used to say: a shroud has no pocket." Meaning, as far as money goes, "You can't take it with you." Whatever possessions one has accumulated during the course of one's life, one cannot take them along on one's final journey.

So even at a major papal Mass in St. Peter's Square, Pope Francis took the humble path, citing his own grandmother. And this, too, is a key to understanding the new pope: He remembers where he came from. He has remained faithful to the faith handed down to him when he was a child. And he is still teaching that faith, the faith of his grandmother, even as he has become the chief teaching authority in the Catholic Church.

Catholics often speak of "the sense of the faithful"—*sensus fidelium*—that feeling of the truth that ordinary people have and that refined theologians, in their speculations, sometimes lose. It is a faith of the heart, as opposed to a faith of the mind. It is a faith of the simple, as opposed to a faith of the complicated. It is a faith that is unswerving and bold, not wavering and hesitating.

For Francis to use the words of his grandmother as his own in a major homily is actually theologically significant. It asserts that the faith of the simple is to be highly regarded, the faith of the lowly to be deeply esteemed and valued. One does not have to have a degree to realize important truths and believe and teach them, Francis seems to be saying. One simply needs to be an ordinary believer.

It is through such believers, he is saying, that the faith is preserved and transmitted. Not through the complexities of the intellectuals, but through the fidelity and trust of the ordinary believers. This is *sensus fidelium*, which preserves and even judges the orthodoxy of the theologians.

Francis, as the Vatican journalist Andrea Tornielli noted in an article just after the Palm Sunday Mass, was referring to his father's mother, Rosa Margherita Vasallo, born in Val Bormida, in northern Italy, in 1881. She married Giovanni Bergoglio, Francis's grandfather, in Turin. She gave birth to the pope's father, Mario, in 1908.

In January 1929, the Bergoglios left Portacomaro, Italy, and set sail for Buenos Aires, where they joined other relatives who had immigrated to Argentina. Despite the hot and humid weather (in the Southern Hemisphere, January is summer), Rosa wore a coat with a fox fur collar, Tornielli noted. In the lining, she carried the revenue from the sale of the family's belongings.

Little Jorge, now the pope, grew up spending part of his day with his grandparents, who taught him some of the Piedmontese dialect and, more important, about the Christian faith.

In a radio interview given in November 2012 to the parish radio station of the slum Villa 21 in Barracas, Argentina, the future pope said: "It was my grandmother who taught me to pray. She left a deep spiritual imprint in me, and used to tell me stories about the saints."

In an interview on the television channel EWTN a year

ago, Cardinal Bergoglio recalled: "Once when I was in the Seminary, my grandmother told me: 'Don't ever forget that you are about to become a priest and celebrating Mass is the most important thing for a priest.' She told me about a mother who told her son, a truly saintly priest: 'Celebrate Mass, every Mass, as if it were your first and last.' "

In the book *El Jesuita*, Cardinal Bergoglio says that he kept a folded text, written by his grandmother, inside his breviary, the two-volume prayer book he always carries with him. The text is a short testament left to her grandchildren. It reads: "May my grandchildren, to whom I have given my whole heart, have a long and happy life, but if pain, sickness, or loss of a loved one should fill them with sadness, may they remember that one breath taken at the Tabernacle, where the greatest and most august martyr is present, and one glance at Mary at the foot of the cross, will act like a balm that is able to heal the deepest and most painful wounds."

PART TWO

The Life That Formed
Pope Francis

CHAPTER 15

....

Family Life: From Buenos Aires to Rome

Birth and Family: 1936–1953

Families form characters, and Pope Francis's tight-knit family formed him.

The new pope was the first of five children, with two younger brothers and two younger sisters—Oscar, Alberto, Marta, and Maria Elena. Only Maria Elena is still living.

As the eldest, he learned to take responsibility, to be decisive, to protect his younger siblings. Maria Elena, who spoke to various newspapers in the days after her brother's election, said: "Jorge taught me to be generous even if it required sacrifice." And she added: "It was Mother and Father who taught us the value of love between family members." She said Jorge was always "very protective towards me, as I was the youngest."

As part of a larger extended family that included his grandparents, Jorge found his identity within a rich fabric of relationships deeply supportive of his identity.

His father's parents, who lived nearby, taught him Italian.

His *nonna* (grandmother) taught him to pray, he has said. Maria Elena recalls that their father would gather the family to pray the Rosary before dinner. Even in his first days as pontiff, her brother was still publicly citing his *nonna* as a source of wisdom, as if her words to him when he was a child had been seared into his heart.

He was born on December 17, 1936, just before Christmas. His mother, Regina, and his father, Mario, named him Jorge, Spanish for George.

His parents were not Argentine or Spanish; they were Italian. They emigrated from the Piedmont region of northern Italy in 1929. So Bergoglio, though born in Latin America and completely fluent in Spanish, is not really Hispanic but rather Italian raised in a Hispanic culture. Thus, when the cardinals elected him pope, they were doing two things at once: taking a dramatic decision to elect "the first pope from the Americas" but also "playing it safe," electing someone born and raised in the context of Italian culture.

Bergoglio's father talked to his children about the "old country," telling them "how life was" in Italy, and what the values there were, Maria Elena told reporters after his election. "He raised us in the love of our native land," she said.

They normally spoke Spanish in the family—"with us he always talked in perfect Castilian," Maria Elena said—but often "in the evenings," when their father and mother would get together with their uncles, "they switched to Italian, preferably to the Piedmontese dialect." The conversation was often about events in Italy, about memories of the beauty of Italy, which "remained a lifelong dream," and about "how much they had suffered during World War I."

They complained about Italian fascism, Maria Elena said. "I remember that my father repeated often that the advent of fascism was the reason that really pushed him to leave. This opposition was important, and shaped Jorge deeply. His sister said this was the reason that her brother could not have been a supporter of the right-wing military regime in Argentina in the 1970s. "My father escaped from Italy because of fascism," she said. "Do you think it is possible that my brother could be an accomplice of a military dictatorship? It would have been like betraying [our father's] memory." During the 1970s, she said, Bergoglio "protected and helped many people who were persecuted by the dictatorship. They were gloomy times and caution was necessary, but his commitment to the victims is proven."

Maria Elena told *La Stampa* newspaper that in 2001, when Pope John Paul II made Bergoglio a cardinal, she went with him back to Italy. "We went to Turin and then to Portacomaro, the town my father left," she said. "The place is gorgeous; we wandered about the nearby hills, then to see the house where my father was born, the garden where he played as a child, the cellars where our uncle made wine: indescribable, an emotion that you can't communicate with words."

The Bergoglio family was not wealthy, but neither was it desperately poor. Mario worked for the Argentine railroad and also, according to a March 27 Reuters report, as an accountant in a hosiery factory. Regina was a full-time housewife, devoting her life to her five children.

"They had a modest existence, being so thrifty that new clothes were seen as dangerously lavish, not once going on holidays and never owning a car," writes Mary O'Regan, author of a thoughtful account of the pope's early life, which appeared in the *Catholic Herald* on March 22. "They were not poor, but were unassuming upper-working-class Italians who considered themselves very fortunate to have secure housing in Flores, an ordinary suburb of Buenos Aires. Many of Mario Bergoglio's fellow workers on the railroads would have lived in shantytowns."

Regina and Mario made sure that their children cleaned their plates at mealtimes—no wasting of good food was allowed. Regina, an excellent cook, taught Jorge. The new pope is also known as an excellent cook.

As the 1930s turned into the 1940s, young Jorge would sit with his mother on Saturdays, listening to opera on the radio. He later reminisced: "It was just the most lovely thing."

The fundamental worldview of the family was shaped by their faith, which brought with it the full round of ordinary Catholic devotions in those years: Sunday Mass—which was in Latin—hymns to Mary in the month of May, the joys of Christmas, and the solemnity of Holy Week. Jorge learned Christian values: humility, honesty, integrity, compassion. And he learned this faith from traditional Catholic nuns wearing traditional habits. His first teacher was Sister Rosa, who helped to shape his mind and heart. Cardinal Bergoglio visited her frequently until her death last year at the age of 101.

In school, Jorge was filled with energy. "Decades before he became Pope Francis, Jorge Bergoglio was a 'little devil' who jumped up and down the stairs of his century-old Buenos Aires school," the establishment's mother superior told Agence France-Press. "The Argentine cardinal memorized his multiplication tables aloud as he skipped steps at the De la Misericordia school, where he celebrated his First Communion at the age of nine," Sister Martha Rabino remembered. The family home was only two blocks away from the school's parish church. "The family went to Mass every Sunday. The mother was very Christian and pious.

[Jorge] learned a lot from her," the seventy-one-year-old Rabino said.

His catechism teacher, Sister Dolores, also had a profound influence on him. "She was another nun that he deeply loved," Sister Martha said. "She was his catechist when he was eight years old, and he never forgot her. He visited her until her death, and when she died he spent the night crying."

Jorge developed his religious vocation at the San Jose de Flores Basilica, where he often led the procession at the start of Holy Week.

And he was thinking of retiring in his childhood neighborhood. He told Sister Martha: "I will spend my last days here." That does not seem very likely now.

Bergoglio has written long letters by hand in very small print to her, she said, always adding the words "pray for me."

Jorge loved to read, but his love of literature eventually gave way to an interest in chemistry, a subject in which he earned a master's degree.

As a young man, he had a wide circle of friends and a girlfriend. He told Francesca Ambrogetti and Sergio Rubin, the authors of his 2010 biography, that his ex-girlfriend "was one of the group of friends I went dancing with. But then I discovered my religious vocation."

The girl, Amalia Damonte, who still lives in Flores, says the future Pope Francis wrote her a love letter when they were twelve. "He told me, 'If you don't marry me, I'll become a priest,'" Damonte said. Her parents broke it off, displeased she was getting such attention from a boy. "Lucky for him, he didn't marry me, and there he is now, as pope!" Damonte told La Nacion of Buenos Aires.

His sister said: "He always played football with his neighborhood friends, and when he grew up he developed a passion for the tango." Bergoglio has been a fan of the San Lorenzo de Almagro soccer team since his childhood. His club membership number is 88,235. On May 24, 2011, the cardinal celebrated the day of María Auxiliadora in the chapel next to San Lorenzo's stadium. "I feel a great joy to celebrate Mass looking through the windows of the Chapel of San Lorenzo's stadium," he said. The team officials published a statement expressing their happiness and pride that Cardinal Bergoglio was the new pope.

The new pope's former classmate Nestor Carabajo told the Argentine newspaper *Clarin* that Jorge was "militantly religious" around the age of fourteen. But the two would also chat about soccer and kick the ball around.

So JORGE BERGOGLIO, in his heart, in his roots, is a *porteño*—the slang term for a native of Buenos Aires. He had a loving, supportive family, he experienced the rich fabric of family relations, with younger brothers and sisters, with uncles chatting with his parents in the evening. All of this gave him a sense of the communion that shared experiences provide. He had strong, deep roots in family, in parish, in community, in culture, in faith.

His home at 531 Membrillar Street—a tree-lined street of large, middle-class homes—is already becoming a site of pilgrimage. "I've seen his work with the poor here for more than a decade," Michaela Döbler, a sixty-nine-year-old resident, told journalists. "He is a divine man who has dedicated a great deal of his time to the poor."

From the pope's family home, it is less than a five-minute drive to one of Argentina's poorest slums, the *villas de emergencias* (crisis communities). The streets are filled with puddles, rubbish, and abandoned cars. The graffiti on the walls include football slogans, gang territory markings, as well as "Jesus" and "Revolution."

But while he was archbishop of Buenos Aires, Bergoglio doubled the number of priests in the slums. One of them, Gustavo Carrara, who was ordained by Bergoglio, said locals were overjoyed that Bergoglio was chosen as pope. "He understands the problems here. . . . Through his career he has always been close to the poor," said Carrara.

Those who know him say Pope Francis is likely to reform the Vatican. Domingo Bresci, a priest who studied with Bergoglio in the fifties and later worked with him in Flores, said the new pope is not a person to take half measures. "Slowly and strategically, he will introduce changes as he becomes more powerful and others become weaker," Bresci told the British newspaper *The Guardian* in a March 16 report. "Until now, no pope has been able to do that. He will be strict on finance. There will be zero tolerance of sexual abuse and homosexual liaisons by priests. This is his style. It comes from Flores."

Yet this man's humility is always present. His sister recalls how in 2005, after he received votes at the papal conclave but was not elected, she and a now-deceased sister, Marta, had joked with their brother. "So you got off the hook," Marta told him. "Yes," Bergoglio replied. "Thank the Lord." This time, before he left, Bergoglio phoned Maria Elena for a quick good-bye. "Pray for me," he told her. "I'll see you when I get back."

Vocation, Studies, and Ordination: 1953–1969

When Jorge Bergoglio finished studying chemistry at age nineteen, his mother asked him what he would study next. "Medicine," he replied, according to Maria Elena as reported by Reuters on March 27.

Bergoglio's mother cleared a storage room in the family's home for him to use as a study, and every day, after his morning job in a lab, he would disappear into the room. One morning, though, his mother found not anatomy or medical texts, but books on theology and Catholicism. Perturbed at this change in course, she asked, "What is this?" Bergoglio responded calmly: "It's medicine for the soul." He had decided to study for the priesthood.

"I don't know what happened," he told an Argentine radio station last year. "But I knew I had to become a priest." And he soon decided to become a Jesuit.

But first he had to deal with a serious infection that led to the surgical removal of his diseased lung.

According to an account in *El Jesuita*, Bergoglio was annoyed by the assurances of people who tried to cheer him. Instead, he found strength in a nun's declaration that he was "imitating Jesus" through suffering. "Pain is not a virtue in itself," Bergoglio told his biographers, "but the way that one handles it can be."

He entered the Society of Jesus as a twenty-one-year-old, which was then considered a slightly late vocation.

He studied liberal arts in Santiago, Chile, and in 1960 earned a degree in philosophy from the Catholic University of Buenos Aires. Between 1964 and 1965 he was a teacher of literature and psychology at Inmaculada high school in the province of Santa Fe, and in 1966 he taught the same courses at the prestigious Colegio del Salvador in Buenos Aires.

In 1967 he returned to his theological studies. He was ordained on December 13, 1969, a few days before he turned thirty-three.

As the first Jesuit pope, Pope Francis can discern God's will and reveal the Gospel in a new way, says a fellow Jesuit, Archbishop Terrence Prendergast of Ottawa, Canada. "He, in a way, embodies the best of what our tradition is about," Prendergast said in a March 21 interview with Deborah Gyapong of *Canadian Catholic News*.

The spiritual disciplines of the Society of Jesus' founder, St. Ignatius of Loyola, help one determine "what God is calling me to do in this particular circumstance at this particular time," Archbishop Prendergast said. "As a Society, we need to let the Holy Spirit guide us in a way that is unique to each one of us. Though Ignatius might not have used the same terms," the archbishop said, "the way God speaks to me is unique to me, as distinct as my fingerprints, my DNA, and the iris[es] of my eyes."

Among the disciplines of Ignatian spirituality is to do an examination of conscience twice a day, to get a sense of one's faults and failures and to "acknowledge where the Lord has been present, where I have acknowledged Him and where I have failed to see Him," Archbishop Prendergast said. There are particular examinations when one is trying to correct a fault or work on developing a virtue. "Somebody who is proud might do humble things; someone who is a doormat might work on becoming assertive," he said.

The goal of the disciplines is "to find equilibrium and balance," Archbishop Prendergast said. "When I am in balance, I can see the movement of spirit and discern whether it is from God or from the enemy of our nature, what Ignatius would call the devil. Ignatius himself would try to find God in all things, to find God in the present moment and respond."

Prendergast said it is natural for Jesuits to be concerned

about the plight of the poor. "Social inequalities had to be addressed" in South America, and "Jesuits went there to use their intellect and their passion for the poor to bring that passion together with the Gospel."

The approach that then father Jorge Bergoglio would have taken is "to always keep the love of the poor coupled with the Gospel," and not go to Marxism, "which sets up class warfare [and] division, not what the Gospel calls for," Prendergast said.

Bergoglio's riding on the subways in Buenos Aires and living in a simple apartment may also have been decisions made out of his Jesuit spirituality, the archbishop said. One makes decisions and continues to live out of them or one might examine them later one and ask "has my living arrangement helped me to grow."

Though the Jesuits are called the Society of Jesus in English, the French and Spanish terms mean "Company" or "Companions" of Jesus, the "band of brothers, the people who share bread together, who share their life together and come out from a common base to serve the world."

The Jesuit and the Priest: 1969–1992

Father Bergoglio completed his final stage of spiritual formation as a Jesuit, tertianship, at Alcalá de Henares, Spain, and took his perpetual vows in the Society of Jesus on April 22, 1973. Having impressed his superiors when he was novice master of the seminary of Villa Barilari in San Miguel, he was only thirty-seven when he was elected superior of the Jesuit province of Argentina. He was named provincial superior of the society in Argentina on July 31, 1973, and served until 1979.

According to Ukrainian Catholic major archbishop Sviatoslav Shevchuk, before becoming a bishop, Bergoglio was mentored by the Salesian Ukrainian Greek Catholic priest Stefan Czmil and, while at the Salesian school, often woke up hours before his classmates so that he could concelebrate Mass with Czmil. This suggests that the new pope has a special sensitivity to the Eastern liturgical tradition, something of great importance in the ecumenical discussions between the Catholic and Orthodox Churches.

Much controversy has arisen over the conduct of Bergoglio during Argentina's 1976–1983 military dictatorship, which cracked down brutally on political opponents. Estimates of the number of people killed and forcibly disappeared during those years range from about 13,000 to more than 30,000.

Citing a case in which two young priests were detained by the military regime, critics say that Bergoglio, who was the highest-ranking Jesuit in the country at the time, did not do enough to support Church workers against the dictatorship. Others, however, have said that he attempted to negotiate behind the scenes for the priests' release, and a spokesman for then cardinal Bergoglio, quoted in the daily newspaper *La Nacion*, called the accusation "old slander."

"I am convinced that it was a 'very grave calumny,'" the respected British Catholic journalist Margaret Hebblethwaite, wife of the late British writer Peter Hebblethwaite, wrote on March 14 in *The Guardian*. "From 1973 to 1979, as Jesuit provincial, Bergoglio had a confrontation with a couple of priests, Orlando Yorio and Francisco Jalics, who were living in a poor barrio and carrying out dangerous work against the military dictatorship. They felt betrayed by Bergoglio because, instead of endorsing their work and protecting them, he demanded they leave the barrio. When they refused, they had to leave the Jesuit order. When they were later 'disappeared' and tortured, it seemed to many that Bergoglio had been siding with the repression. It was the kind of complex situation that is capable of multiple interpretations, but it is far more likely Bergoglio was trying to save their lives."

Bergoglio has described his efforts to hide or help some targets flee, including one who the provincial said resembled him and crossed the northern border dressed as a priest and carrying Bergoglio's identity card.

What is certain is that during the "Dirty War" he demanded the absolute obedience and political neutrality of his priests, something that many of them greatly resented. The Jesuit order was showing cracks because of infighting, as many priests were seduced by a blend of Marxism and Liberation Theology, and rebelled against the traditional nature of a priestly vocation.

Father Bergoglio's six years as a leader in the Jesuit community were hard on his nerves, and in 1980 he returned to the seminary in San Miguel as rector. Going from provincial superior to rector was seen as a self-imposed demotion, but he remained in this post until 1986. He put his culinary talent to use cooking for the students. On hearing the compliment that he was a good chef, he replied: "Well, nobody has died yet from my cooking."

A key awakening in his spiritual life happened in 1985, when he attended a Rosary that was being led by Pope John Paul II. He described it in these words:

> In the middle of the prayer I became distracted, looking at the figure of the Pope: his piety, his devotion was a witness . . . and the time drifted

away, and I began to imagine the young priest, the
seminarian, the poet, the worker, the child from
Wadowice . . . in the same position in which he
knelt at that moment, reciting *Ave Maria* after *Ave
Maria*. His witness struck me. . . . I felt that this man,
chosen to lead the Church, was following a path up
to his Mother in the sky, a path set out on from his
childhood. And I became aware of the density of
the words of the Mother of Guadalupe to St. Juan
Diego: "Don't be afraid, am I not perhaps your
mother?" I understood the presence of Mary in the
life of the Pope.

Also in the 1980s, Bergoglio spent several months at the
Sankt Georgen Graduate School of Philosophy and Theology in Frankfurt, Germany, considering possible dissertation
topics, before returning to Argentina to serve as a confessor
and spiritual director to the Jesuit community in Córdoba.

The Bishop and a Deepening
Global Vision: 1992–2001

When many believed that the tall, thin, intellectual
priest would end his days teaching, writing, and
spending several hours in the confessional, Cardinal Antonio Quarracino called Father Bergoglio to Buenos Aires in
1990.

In May 1992, he was appointed one of three auxiliary
bishops of Buenos Aires. He kept a low profile, spending
most of his time caring for the Catholic university, coun-
seling priests, and preaching and hearing confessions. On
June 3, 1997, Bergoglio was named coadjutor archbishop. He

was installed as the new archbishop of Buenos Aires on February 28, 1998.

He became an outspoken opponent of abortion, divorce, and euthanasia. "A pregnant woman is not carrying a toothbrush in her womb, or a tumor," he once said. "Science shows us that the entire genetic code is present from the moment of conception. It's not therefore a religious issue, but scientifically based morality, because we are in the presence of a human being." He has also said that women who terminate their pregnancies suffer "giant dramas" of conscience. He also defended the withholding of Communion from divorcés.

During his time as archbishop in his home city, his humility and identification with the people were evident as he traveled to the poorer parts of Buenos Aires delivering Mass. Bergoglio created many new parishes, restructured administrative offices, took personal care of the seminary, and started new pastoral projects, such as a commission for divorced people. He mediated in almost all social or political conflicts in the city. Argentina's priests ordained since 1998 are sometimes described as "the Bergoglio generation."

He also did something simple but revolutionary: he set up a phone line exclusively for priests and encouraged them to use it, day or night.

He spent his days traveling around the diocese, so that he could keep poor people company, help out in soup kitchens, and visit AIDS victims. His schedule was grueling, and one of his few luxuries was taking refuge in a good novel.

The poor children who were his peers when he was a youngster were in his thoughts, and he was determined to use his prominence as a bishop to better the lot of the impoverished, as opposed to rubbing shoulders with the Argentine elite. So he rode the bus, visited the poor, lived in a simple apartment, and cooked his own meals. To many in Buenos Aires, he was known simply as Father Jorge.

The Cardinal and the Global Church: 2001–2013

In 2001, Pope John Paul II named Bergoglio a cardinal, and suddenly he was on the global stage.

When Pope John Paul II died, in 2005, Bergoglio attended the conclave to elect his successor, and was nearly elected himself. An article published in September 2005 by *Limes*, a respected Italian journal on geopolitics, has reconstructed the outlines of what took place. On each of the four ballots the prelate receiving the second-highest number of votes was Cardinal Jorge Mario Bergoglio. *Limes* said its information came from the diary of an anonymous cardinal who, while acknowledging he was violating his oath of secrecy, felt the conclave votes should be part of the historical record.

The cardinal said that on the first ballot, Cardinal Ratzinger received 47 votes. The other cardinals who got more than one vote on the first ballot were Cardinal Bergoglio with 10 votes; retired Italian cardinal Carlo Maria Martini of Milan, 9; Italian cardinal Camillo Ruini, papal vicar of Rome, 6; Cardinal Angelo Sodano, Vatican secretary of state, 4; Honduran cardinal Oscar Rodriguez Maradiaga of Tegucigalpa, 3; and Italian cardinal Dionigi Tettamanzi of Milan, 2.

"The real surprise on the first ballot" was the support for Cardinal Bergoglio, the magazine said.

The diary writer said the Argentinian was supported by cardinals "Karl Lehmann, president of the German episcopal conference, and Godfried Danneels, archbishop of Brussels, who led a significant squad of U.S. and Latin American cardinals," in addition to a couple of Vatican officials.

The diarist said that even before the cardinals left the Sistine Chapel for lunch "there were the first comments and contacts. There was great concern among the cardinals who hoped for the election of Cardinal Ratzinger."

On the fourth and final ballot, which began at 4:30 P.M., Cardinal Ratzinger received eighty-four votes, seven more than were needed. Cardinal Bergoglio had twenty-six votes, the diarist said.

Limes said it is not known why some of Cardinal Bergoglio's supporters switched their votes. "Perhaps they simply thought it was inopportune to hope for a prolonged delay with the risk of a serious division without a real and convincing alternative to [Cardinal] Ratzinger," the magazine said.

So Bergoglio was not elected and returned to Buenos Aires.

In 2006, Bergoglio criticized an Argentine proposal to legalize abortion under certain circumstances as part of a wide-ranging legal reform. He accused the government of lacking respect for the values held by the majority of Argentinians and of trying to convince the Catholic Church "to waver in our defense of the dignity of the person."

In 2010, when Argentina considered legislation to become the first Latin American country to permit same-sex marriage, Cardinal Bergoglio encouraged clergy across the country to tell Catholics to protest the legislation because it could "seriously injure the family." On June 22, 2010, Cardinal Bergoglio wrote a letter to the Carmelites of his diocese regarding the legal redefinition of marriage.

The Argentine people must face, in the next few weeks, a situation whose result may gravely harm the family. It is the bill on matrimony of persons of the same gender. The identity of the family, and its survival, are in jeopardy here: father, mother, and children. The life of so many children who will be discriminated beforehand due to the lack of human maturity that God willed them to have with a father and a mother is in jeopardy. A clear rejection of the law of God, engraved in our hearts, is in jeopardy.

Here, the envy of the Devil, through which sin entered the world, is also present, and deceitfully intends to destroy the image of God: man and woman, who receive the mandate to grow, multiply, and conquer the earth. Let us not be naive: it is not a simple political struggle; it is an intention [which is] destructive of the plan of God. It is not a mere legislative project (this is a mere instrument), but rather a "move" of the father of lies who wishes to confuse and deceive the children of God.

I turn to you and ask from you prayer and sacrifice. . . . Cry out to the Lord that he may send his Spirit to the Senators who are to place their votes. That they may not do it moved by error or by circumstantial matters, but rather according to what the natural law and the law of God tell them. Pray for them, for their families; that the Lord may visit, strengthen, and console them. Pray that they may do great good for the Nation.

Pope Francis

The role Francis—who now has full authority in the Church, even over Pope Emeritus Benedict—assigns to his living predecessor will be the first great decisions of his pontificate. The cardinals who have elected him expect the new pope to intervene immediately and decisively to restore order in the Curia. So the second great decision of the new pontificate will be the choice of a new secretary of state. And the third great decision of Pope Francis will be to choose the means to revive the Christian faith where it is almost extinguished and to germinate it where it has not yet arrived.

Francis is the first pope to have been ordained a priest after the Second Vatican Council (1962–1965). Pope Benedict XVI will most likely be the last pope who was a priest in the preconciliar era and was connected with the council.

At his first appearance on the loggia of St. Peter's Basilica, the newly elected Jorge Mario Bergoglio wanted two cardinals with him: at his right his vicar for the diocese of Rome, Agostino Vallini, and at his left his Brazilian friend Cláudio Hummes, a Franciscan. The new pope wants to be the bishop of Rome, going from church to church, from the center to the periphery, "for the evangelization of this city that is so beautiful," as he said in his very first remarks on March 13. He wishes to be in continual, direct contact with the people of his diocese, which he considers to be his "Bride."

Words of Inspiration

As reported in *La Nacion* in Beunos Aires on March 21, Jorge Bergoglio, during his time as archbishop, had a selection of books on his nightstand that may give a clue about his predilections. Of course, they do not constitute all the readings of Pope Francis, but they are the texts that he recommends to people who place themselves under his spiritual guidance.

The book that perhaps excites the new pontiff the most is *The Lord*, by the famous theologian and historian Romano Guardini.

Another favorite author is Spaniard Dolores Aleixandre. She is a sister of the Sacred Heart of Jesus and a theologian at the University of Comillas. Her titles most mentioned by the pope are *Baptized with Fire* [*Bautizados con fuego*] and *Telling Jesus* [*Contar a Jesús*].

Cardinal François-Xavier Nguyen Van Thuan, who spent thirteen years in the prisons of the Vietnamese regime and is, as is the new pope, a fervent devotee of St. Thérèse of Lisieux, is one of his other favorites.

The famous Cardinal Carlo Maria Martini (1927–2012), a Jesuit, as is the pope, appears with the biblical commentary *Words to Live By* [*Parole per vivere*] and *Effata*, dedicated to social communication.

Another favorite author of Francis is the Dutch priest Henri Nouwen, chaplain of the L'Arche Daybreak community and author of *The Return of the Prodigal Son* among many other books.

Paths of Hope [*Wege zur Freiheit*], a sort of self-help book, is another recommended by the new pope. Its author is the Benedictine Anselm Grün, who is an expert in finance and business administration.

The Spanish priest José Luis Martín Descalzo, who died in 1991, comes up with his book *Testament of the Lonely Bird* [*Testamento del pájaro solitario*].

Finally, there is Ethel Mannin, an English anarchist

pacifist and the author of *Late Have I Loved Thee*, who had a well-known relationship with Bertrand Russell, one of the masters of atheism.

The new pope's favorite film is said to be *Babette's Feast*, the story of a woman who spends all of her inheritance on one beautiful, extravagant feast for her neighbors.

ALMOST SIXTY years have passed since the seventeen-year-old Jorge Bergoglio first felt the tug of a vocation that has led him to the highest office in the Church. Speaking before his installation, his sister Maria Elena told journalists, "The main concern I have for my brother is not to leave him alone. Francis is asking the Church to resume her journey, but we, the faithful, must walk with him."

CHAPTER 16

....

Five of Pope Francis's
Spiritual Guides

By reading some of his writings, and studying some of his conversations, we can find hints about what is important to Pope Francis, what nourishes him, what orients him. We quickly discover that there are five "spiritual guides," five figures who are important in understanding his identity and destiny as a man, a priest, and now a pope.

Jonah

But he answered and said unto them, An evil and adulterous generation seeketh after a sign; and there shall no sign be given to it, but the sign of the prophet Jonas:

For as Jonas was three days and three nights in the whale's belly; so shall the Son of man be three days and three nights in the heart of the earth.

The men of Nineveh shall rise in judgment with this generation, and shall condemn it: because they repented at the preaching of Jonas; and, behold, a greater than Jonas is here. —*Matthew 12:39–41*

The first of Pope Francis's spiritual guides is the Hebrew prophet Jonah. This may seem peculiar—Jonah is not often mentioned among the great spiritual guides for modern Christians. But Jonah has been important as a warning sign for the new pope's own spirituality. In a November 2007 interview with Stefania Falasca of *30 Giorni* magazine, then cardinal Jorge Bergoglio explained why.

Bergoglio and Falasca were discussing why the proclamation of the Christian Good News so often doesn't seem to have much effect. People aren't excited to hear the message the Church generally preaches, they noted.

And since the greatest problem facing the Church today is the loss of the faith, the loss of interest in the faith, part of the greatest problem the pope faces is how to make the Good News attractive again.

As they talked, Bergoglio mentioned how the faith survived for centuries in Japan, even without priests. In that island country, "the faith had remained intact through the gifts of grace that had gladdened the life of a laity who had received only baptism and had also lived their apostolic mission in virtue of baptism alone. One must not be afraid of depending only on His tenderness. . . . Do you know the biblical episode of the prophet Jonah?"

"I don't remember it," Falasca said. "Tell us."

"Jonah had everything clear," Bergoglio said. "He had clear ideas about God, very clear ideas about good and evil. On what God does and on what He wants, on who is faithful to the Covenant and who instead is outside the Covenant. He had the 'recipe' for being a good prophet." In other words, Bergoglio was saying, this "prophet" had started to get in the way of the very message he was supposed to proclaim, because of his own pride and presuppositions.

But then "God broke into his life like a torrent," Bergoglio said. "He sent him to Nineveh. Nineveh was the symbol of all the separated, the lost, of all the 'peripheries' of humanity. Of all those who are outside, forlorn." So Jonah faced a task that is very similar to the task facing a Christian today, to the task facing a pope today. He was called by God to preach to a place where few, or none, would even wish to listen to him. "Jonah saw that the task set on him was only to tell all those people that the arms of God were still open, that the patience of God was there and waiting, to heal them with His forgiveness and nourish them with His tenderness," Bergoglio said. "Only for that had God sent him. God sent him to Nineveh, but Jonah instead ran off in the opposite direction, toward Tarsus."

"Running away from a difficult mission," said Falasca. But . . .

"No," said Bergoglio. "What Jonah was fleeing was not so much Nineveh, as the boundless love of God for those people." Bergoglio does not see, on the superficial level, that Jonah was avoiding a difficult assignment. He sees that Jonah was scandalized by God's love for people unworthy of his love. "It was that that didn't come into his plans," Bergoglio continued. "God had come once . . . 'and I'll see to the rest': that's what Jonah told himself. He wanted to do things his way, he wanted to steer it all. His stubbornness shut him in his own structures of evaluation, in his preordained methods, in his righteous opinions. He had fenced his soul off with the barbed wire of those certainties that instead of giving freedom with God and opening horizons of greater service to others, had finished by deafening his heart. How the isolated conscience hardens the heart! Jonah no longer knew that God leads His people with the heart of a Father."

And Falasca got the point: "A great many of us can identify with Jonah," she said.

And she was right. Very many of us like our own mis-
sions, our own day-to-day lives, to be fully "ours," under our
control. But Bergoglio saw a danger in this.

"Our certainties can become a wall, a jail that imprisons
the Holy Spirit," he said. "Those who isolate their conscience
from the path of the people of God don't know the joy of
the Holy Spirit that sustains hope. That is the risk run by
the isolated conscience. Of those who from the closed world
of their Tarsus complain about everything or, feeling their
identity threatened, launch themselves into battles only in
the end to be still more self-concerned and self-referential."

Bergoglio is speaking of the danger that human beings,
with their notions and prejudices can "quench" the Spirit.
We must remain open to the leading of the Spirit, even—or
perhaps especially—when we think that we are doing everything right.

"What should one do?" Falasca asked.

And Bergoglio was ready with a reply. "Look at our
people, not for what they should be, but for what they are,
and see what is necessary," he said. "Without preconceptions
and recipes, but with generous openness. God spoke for the
wounds and for the frailties. Allow the Lord to speak. . . . In
a world that we can't manage to interest with the words we
speak, the only thing that can be of interest is His presence
that loves us, that saves us. The apostolic fervor should be
renewed so that it bears witness to Him who has loved us
from the beginning."

And then Falasca, who understood that Bergoglio was
describing a situation in which the Church's message—
which is not a verbal message but the bearing of witness to

a personal, divine reality—was being muffled, almost displaced, asked: "For you, then, what is the worst thing that can happen in the Church?"

And Bergoglio answered: "It is what De Lubac calls 'spiritual worldliness.' It is the greatest danger for the Church, for us, who are in the Church. 'It is worse,' says De Lubac, 'more disastrous than that shameful leprosy that disfigured the beloved Bride at the time of the corrupt Popes.' Spiritual worldliness is putting oneself at the center. It is what Jesus saw going on among the Pharisees: 'You who glorify yourselves. Who give glory to yourselves, each one to the other.'"

In these powerful words, Bergoglio, already in 2007, was making clear his diagnosis of the malady harming the Church. He was saying there is a malady even more devastating than the sin and corruption of the Renaissance popes, with their mistresses and children. Worse than that is a type of religiosity that hardens the heart in self-contentedness and makes it impossible for the Spirit to act because all the plans are already made by human beings.

Mary

We have already spoken about Pope Francis's Marian devotion. He invoked Mary in each of his early homilies, he visited the icon of Mary and the child Jesus in St. Mary Major as the first act of his papacy, he has prayed five decades of the Rosary daily since 1985, and he brought an icon of Mary to Pope Emeritus Benedict when they met on March 23. So there is no need to repeat here that Pope Francis has a profound Marian devotion. There is simply a need to stress that Mary, the "humble handmaid of the Lord," is the source of that "teaching of humility" that Francis has

been trying to live out all of his adult life, and to such astonishing effect in the first two weeks of his papacy.

And this has been noticed. When Metropolitan Hilarion
Alfeyev of the Russian Orthodox Church gave that icon of
the Virgin Mary to Pope Francis on March 20, Hilarion
said: "The first steps of Your Holiness after the election
were marked by humbleness."

And this path of humility, a Marian path, is the path
Francis has said he will pursue to the end, no matter how
many eyebrows it raises. Because this is the path that he believes will bring forth great fruit, not due to his merit but
due to the opening his own humility will give to the action
of the Spirit.

Pope Francis's emphasis on the Virgin Mary is "traditional" though it leads him to take actions that may appear
"revolutionary." This is, in fact, the secret of his spirituality.
It is both traditional and revolutionary at once, because it is
humble and Marian, and yet open to the intense promptings
of the Spirit. And the Spirit can prompt revolutionary things,
things not usually thought of by ecclesial professionals.

This Marian spirituality is, of course, quite popular in
the Spanish-speaking world. There is even a special Marian devotion that, especially in Argentina and Brazil, has
become extremely popular in recent years, partly thanks to
Pope Francis himself.

There is an eighteenth-century German painting that de-
picts the Virgin Mary taking the knots out of a long white
ribbon. The image, which has been kept in the same church
in Augsburg for three hundred years, is barely known in its
home country. But in South America, it has become ubiq-
uitous. At least two Mary Untier of Knots churches have
been opened in the past year, pictures of this image are often

distributed in the streets, and you can even buy "Untier of Knots starter kits" containing a novena, a prayer sheet, a string of beads, and a bracelet.

It is estimated that the Catholic Church has about two thousand titles for the Virgin Mary. And Mary Untier of Knots, formerly one of the least known, is now rapidly growing in importance.

The story of Mary Untier of Knots began in the early 1700s, when Johann Schmittdner was commissioned to paint an interpretation of the Virgin Mary. The image—called *Maria Knotenlöserin* in German—was put on the altar of the St. Peter am Perlach church in Augsburg.

More than twenty years ago, when he was studying for a few months in Germany, then father Bergoglio saw the image. He brought a copy of it back to Argentina, where it came to be venerated. A chapel in its honor was inaugurated in 2012 in Formosa, on the Paraguay border. In 2011 the image found its way to Brazil. There are now Untier of Knots worship centers in five states and, in September 2012, a church was founded in Buzios, near Rio de Janeiro. Regina Novaes, of Rio's Institute of Religious Studies, says that the Mary Untier of Knots "attracts people with small problems."

This devotion fits with Pope Francis's general spirituality. He is attracted to saints like Juan Diego of Guadalupe and Francis of Assisi: small, poor men with great devotion to the Mother of God. And those two humble saints brought about the greatest moments of evangelization in the history of the Church.

In this perspective, Francis's devotion to Mary, and to Mary Untier of Knots, may be a clue to his strategy to entrust to Mary the project of the "new evangelization," which has been spoken of so continually for the past twenty years in the Catholic Church. Evangelization always depends on the mediating intercessions of the Mother of God. This may very well mean that Francis will choose to carry out special, unprecedented Marian initiatives, to bring the news of Christ to a technologically advanced, financially prosperous, highly secularized world.

My hunch is that Pope Francis believes true devotion to Mary is the key to both personal conversion and conversion of the entire world to Christ the King. I hope that the new pontiff will bear that warm "Marian glow" carried by popes Pius IX, Leo XIII, St. Pius X, Pius XII, and John Paul II. Perhaps when the secular press speak of "humility" in Pope Francis, what they really see is a pontiff who is quietly Marian. Time will tell.

Ignatius of Loyola

> Take, Lord, and receive all my liberty, my memory, my
> understanding, and my entire will, all I have and possess;
> you have given me, I now give it back to you, O Lord;
> all is yours, dispose of it according to your will; give me
> only your love and your grace; that is enough for me.
> —*Prayer of St. Ignatius*

We know that Pope Francis is a member of the Jesuit order, the Society of Jesus, founded by St. Ignatius. So there is no doubt that the new pope has been deeply influenced by the thought and example of Ignatius. But what does this mean in practice?

All followers of Ignatian spirituality are supposed to use certain spiritual exercises aimed at enabling them to discern their path and to make good decisions.

The Daily Examen is "a technique of prayerful reflection on the events of the day in order to detect God's presence and discern his direction for us," according to a Jesuit manual. "The Examen is an ancient practice in the Church that can help us see God's hand at work in our whole experience." So the very bedrock of this spirituality is to see the divine will in the events of daily life, to see the traces or tracks of God's presence, even if he himself is invisible, hidden.

St. Ignatius thought that the examen was a gift that came directly from God, and that God wanted it to be shared as widely as possible. One of the few rules of prayer that Ignatius made was the requirement that Jesuits practice the examen twice daily—at noon and at the end of the day. It's a habit that Jesuits, and many other Christians, practice to this day.

Here is one simple version of the Daily Examen, drawn from a Jesuit website:

1. Become aware of God's presence.
2. Review the day with gratitude.
3. Pay attention to your emotions.
4. Choose one feature of the day and pray from it.
5. Look toward tomorrow.

This is not like the normal examination of conscience that one performs before going to confess one's sins. The purpose of the examen is to put away the clutter of the world and focus your mind and thoughts on "how God sees your life."

Here are the steps in a little greater detail:

1. *Become aware of God's presence.* Look back on the events of the day in the company of the Holy Spirit. The day

may seem confusing to you—a blur, a jumble, a muddle. Ask God to bring clarity and understanding to it.

2. *Review the day with gratitude.* Gratitude is the foundation of our relationship with God. Walk through your day in the presence of God and note its joys and delights. Focus on the day's gifts. Look at the work you did, the people you interacted with. What did you receive from these people? What did you give them? Pay attention to little things—the food you ate, the sights you saw, and other seemingly small pleasures. God is in the details.

3. *Pay attention to your emotions.* One of St. Ignatius's great insights was that we detect the presence of the Spirit of God in the movements of our emotions. Reflect on the feelings you experienced during the day. Boredom? Elation? Resentment? Compassion? Anger? Confidence? What is God saying through these feelings?

God will most likely show you some ways that you fell short. Make note of these sins and faults. But look deeply for other implications. Does a feeling of frustration perhaps mean that God wants you to consider a new direction in some area of your work? Are you concerned about a friend? Perhaps you should reach out to her in some way.

4. *Choose one feature of the day and pray from it.* Ask the Holy Spirit to direct you to something during the day that is particularly important. It may involve a feeling—positive or negative. It may be a significant encounter with another person or a vivid moment of pleasure or peace. Or it may be something that seems rather insignificant. Look at it. Pray about it. Allow the prayer—whether

intercession, praise, repentance, or gratitude—to arise
spontaneously from your heart.

5. *Look toward tomorrow.* Ask God to give you light for tomorrow's challenges. Pay attention to the feelings that
surface as you survey what's coming up. Are you doubt-
ful? Cheerful? Apprehensive? Full of delighted anticipation? Allow these feelings to turn into prayer. Seek
God's guidance. Ask him for help and understanding.
Pray for hope.

St. Ignatius encouraged people to talk to Jesus like a
friend. End your Daily Examen with a conversation with
Jesus. Ask forgiveness for your sins. Ask for his protection
and help. Ask for his wisdom about the questions you have
and the problems you face. Do all this in the spirit of gratitude. Your life is a gift, and it is adorned with gifts from
God. End the Daily Examen with the Our Father.

Father Michael Kelly, S.J., of Bangkok, has written an
essay on Francis's Ignatian spirituality. He writes, "Much
has been made of the impressions Pope Francis has created
by his ordinary, everyday activities: catching buses, using a
telephone to make his own calls, not dressing in all the fine
drapery usually worn by popes, treating people respectfully
as he did the journalists, celebrating the Holy Thursday
Mass in a Roman prison. As Jorge Bergoglio, the current
pope's first and then recurrent experience of ministry as a
Jesuit was his making and directing the Spiritual Exercises
of St. Ignatius Loyola, the founder of the Jesuits. Twice at
least he has made the thirty-day retreat, and he has also
guided others over many years through that experience. The
Exercises are at once a school of prayer and an experience

with one purpose—making decisions about directions in life."

At the heart of this spirituality is "a constant preoccupation with the person of Jesus—in his teaching and preaching in word and indeed climaxing in prolonged meditation on his death and resurrection. The helpless surrender of Jesus to God's love on Calvary and the astonishing reversal that comes with the Resurrection are seen through not only Jesus' eyes but also in the Calvaries and resurrections of the retreatant's life."

Don Luigi Giussani

> May I take the liberty of thanking all who are present, for me a great sign of esteem for Him who, through the frailty of our person, makes Himself visible, audible, and tangible in the world. —*Don Luigi Giussani, founder of the Communion and Liberation movement, to Cardinal Bergoglio, who was presenting Giussani's book on the attractiveness of Christ to a group in Buenos Aires in 1999*

Pope Francis preached on his first visit to a parish that "this is the Lord's most powerful message: mercy." His motto, *"Miserando atque eligendo"* (By having mercy and by choosing him) is about Jesus' mercy toward sinners.

On April 7, 2001, at the Buenos Aires International Book Fair, then archbishop Jorge Bergoglio presented the Spanish edition of Don Luigi Giussani's book *L'attrattiva Gesù* [The Attraction that is Jesus]. In his talk, he used the phrase discussed elsewhere in this book: "The locus of the encounter is the caress of the mercy of Jesus Christ on my sin."

The origins of some of Pope Francis's thought about Christ, about God's mercy, about the forgiveness of sins and the personal encounter with Jesus, are in the thought of Don Luigi Giussani and also Don Giacomo Tantardini, leaders of the Communion and Liberation group in Rome for many years. Giussani died in February 2005, and then cardinal Ratzinger celebrated his funeral Mass and delivered an important homily on the occasion, just days before his election as Pope Benedict XVI. Tantardini died in April 2012, and then cardinal Bergoglio wrote a eulogy in his memory, just a few months before his election as Pope Francis.

Faithful to his personal style, in his presentation of Giussani's book the cardinal was very brief and clear. In thirty-five minutes, he presented the most important sections of the dialogues in *L'attrattiva Gesù* and compared some of Don Giussani's statements to others by St. Thérèse of Lisieux and St. Augustine.

Here is the text of this talk:

> I agreed to present this book by Father Giussani
> for two reasons. The first and more personal one
> is the good that this man has done me, in my life
> as a priest, through the reading of his books and
> articles. The second reason is that I am convinced
> that his thought is profoundly human and reaches
> man's innermost longings. I daresay that this is the
> most profound, and at the same time understand-
> able, phenomenology of nostalgia as a transcendental
> fact. There is a phenomenology of nostalgia, *nóstos
> algos*, feeling being called home, the experience of

feeling attracted to what is most proper for us, most
consonant with our being. In the context of Father
Giussani's reflections, we encounter instances of a
real phenomenology of nostalgia.

The book presented today, *El atractivo de Jesucristo*,
is not a theological treatise, it is a dialogue of
friendship; these are table conversations between
Father Giussani and his disciples. It is not a book
for intellectuals, but for common men and women.
It is the description of that initial experience, which
I shall refer to later on, of wonder which arises in
dialogue about daily experience that is provoked and
fascinated by the exceptionally human and divine
presence and gaze of Jesus Christ. It is the story of
a personal relationship—intense, mysterious, and
concrete at the same time—of an impassioned and
intelligent affection for the person of Jesus, and this
enables Father Giussani to come to the threshold,
as it were, of Mystery, to speak familiarly and
intimately with Mystery.

Everything in our life, today just as in Jesus' time,
begins with an encounter. An encounter with this
Man, the carpenter of Nazareth, a man like all men
and yet different. The first ones, John, Andrew, and
Simon, felt themselves to be looked at into their very
depths, read in their innermost being, and in them
sprang forth a surprise, a wonder that instantly made
them feel bound to Him, made them feel different.

When Jesus asked Peter, "Do you love Me?" his
"Yes" was not the result of an effort of will, it was
not the fruit of a "decision" made by the young
man Simon: it was the emergence, the coming to the

surface of an entire vein of tenderness and adherence that made sense because of the esteem he had for Him—therefore an act of reason; it was a reasonable act, which is why he couldn't not say "Yes."

We cannot understand this dynamic of encounter which brings forth wonder and adherence if it has not been triggered—forgive me the use of this word—by mercy. Only someone who has encountered mercy, who has been caressed by the tenderness of mercy, is happy and comfortable with the Lord. I beg the theologians who are present not to turn me in to the Sant'Uffizio or to the Inquisition; however, forcing things a bit, I dare to say that the privileged locus of the encounter is the caress of the mercy of Jesus Christ on my sin.

In front of this merciful embrace—and I continue along the lines of Giussani's thought—we feel a real desire to respond, to change, to correspond; a new morality arises. We posit the ethical problem, an ethics which is born of the encounter, of this encounter which we have described up to now. Christian morality is not a titanic effort of the will, the effort of someone who decides to be consistent and succeeds, a solitary challenge in the face of the world. No. Christian morality is simply a response. It is the heartfelt response to a surprising, unforeseeable, "unjust" mercy (I shall return to this adjective). The surprising, unforeseeable, "unjust" mercy, using purely human criteria, of one who knows me, knows my betrayals and loves me just the same, appreciates me, embraces me, calls me again, hopes in me, and expects from me. This is why the

Christian conception of morality is a revolution; it
is not a never falling down but an always getting up
again.

As we shall see, this authentic, in a Christian
sense, conception of morality which Giussani
presents has nothing to do with the spiritualistic-
type quietisms of which the shelves of the religious
supermarkets of today are full. Trickery. Nor
with the Pelagianism so fashionable today in its
different, sophisticated manifestations. Pelagianism,
underneath it all, is a remake of the Tower of Babel.
The spiritualistic quietisms are efforts at prayer
and immanent spirituality which never go beyond
themselves.

Jesus is encountered, just as two thousand years
ago, in a human presence, the Church, the company
of those whom He assimilates to Himself, His Body,
the sign and sacrament of His Presence. Reading this
book, one is amazed and filled with admiration at
the sight of such a personal and profound relationship with Jesus, and thinks it is unlikely to happen
to him. When people say to Father Giussani "How
brave one has to be to say 'Yes' to Christ!" or "This
objection comes to my mind: it is evident that Father
Giussani loves Jesus and I don't love Him in the
same way," Giussani answers, "Why do you oppose
what you think you don't have to what you think I
have? I have this yes, only this, and it would not cost
you one iota more than it costs me. . . . Say 'Yes' to
Jesus. If I foresaw that tomorrow I would offend
Him a thousand times, I would still say it." Thérèse

of Lisieux says almost exactly the same thing: "I say it, because if I did not say 'Yes' to Jesus, I could not say 'Yes' to the stars in the sky or to your hair, the hairs on your head. . . ." Nothing could be simpler: "I don't know how it is, I don't know how it might be: I know that I have to say 'Yes.' I can't not say it," and reasonably; that is to say, at every moment in his reflections in this book, Giussani has recourse to the reasonableness of experience.

It is a question of starting to say "Yes" to Christ, and saying it often. It is impossible to desire it without asking for it. And if someone starts to ask for it, then he begins to change. Besides, if someone asks for it, it is because in the depths of his being he feels attracted, called, looked at, awaited. This is the experience of Augustine: there from the depths of my being, something attracts me toward Someone who looked for me first, is waiting for me first, is the almond flower of the prophets, the first to bloom in spring. It is the quality which God possesses and which I take the liberty of defining by using a Buenos Aires word: God, in this case Jesus Christ, always *primerea*, goes ahead of us. When we arrive, He is already there waiting.

He who encounters Jesus Christ feels the impulse to witness Him or to give witness of what he has encountered, and this is the Christian calling. To go and give witness. You can't convince anybody. The encounter occurs. You can prove that God exists, but you will never be able, using the force of persuasion, to make anyone encounter God. This is pure grace.

Pure grace. In history, from its very beginning until today, grace always *primerea*, grace always comes first, then comes all the rest.

Francis

Lord, make me an instrument of your peace,
Where there is hatred, let me sow love;
Where there is injury, pardon;
Where there is doubt, faith;
Where there is despair, hope;
Where there is darkness, light;
Where there is sadness, joy.
O Divine Master,
grant that I may not so much seek to be consoled, as to console;
to be understood, as to understand;
to be loved, as to love.
For it is in giving that we receive.
It is in pardoning that we are pardoned,
and it is in dying that we are born to Eternal Life. Amen.
—Prayer of St. Francis

The final "spiritual guide" for Pope Francis is the man whose name he chose: St. Francis of Assisi.

Why did he choose the name of the one among all the saints who may have least wanted to be a pope—St. Francis? It would seem to be because of both Francis's humility and burning love for Jesus and the reality that the figure of Francis conveys to untold millions. Certainly anyone looking more closely will quickly see that the "Franciscan spirit" was already to a large extent present in the life of Father, Bishop, Archbishop, and Cardinal Bergoglio.

What is the "Franciscan spirit"? In a phrase: to be Christlike. Many commentators have told audiences and readers that if they want a picture of the "Franciscan spirit" they should read G. K. Chesterton's life of St. Francis. But a much briefer source for perhaps an even more incisive portrait of Francis's holiness is one chapter authored by a man Bergoglio greatly admires: Joseph Ratzinger, Pope Benedict XVI.

In chapter 4 of volume 1 of *Jesus of Nazareth*, Ratzinger writes on the Sermon on the Mount, and the Beatitudes, and puts Francis's total dedication to following Jesus in a line he traces from the Old Testament to the apostles, especially St. Paul. The center of this agape love is to become Christlike, and he finds St. Francis "the figure whom the history of faith offers us as the most intensely lived illustration" of the first Beatitude: "Blessed are the poor in spirit, theirs is the Kingdom of Heaven." He adds, "Francis of Assisi was gripped in an utterly radical way by the promise of the first Beatitude, to the point that he even gave away his garments and let himself be clothed anew by the bishop, the representative of God's fatherly goodness, through which the lilies of the field were clad in robes finer than Solomon's (cf. Mt 6:28–29)." Francis, Ratzinger tells us, "was perfectly conformed to the wounds of the stigmata, so perfectly that from then on he truly no longer lived as himself, but as one reborn, totally from and in Jesus Christ."

If Pope John Paul II's unfailing charge to all believers was: "Be not afraid. . . . Be not afraid to open your hearts to the inexpressible love of Christ," Pope Francis's call to all seekers of the highest spirituality may well urge his listeners to strive to imitate the kind of love the little poor man of Assisi showed for Jesus and his neighbor.

Cardinal Hummes expressed himself this way two days

after the election of Bergoglio as pope: "Very many are awaiting a reform of the Curia and I am certain that he will do it, in the light of the essentiality, the simplicity and humility asked for by the Gospel. Always in the footsteps of the saint whose name he has taken. St. Francis had a great love for the hierarchical church, for the Pope: he wanted his friars to be Catholics and to obey the 'Lord pope,' as he put it."

This reference to Francis is not trivial for a pope who is expected to "repair the Church."

St. Francis was also probably the most Marian saint who ever lived. His entire life was consecrated to Mary. He is probably the first saint to identify Mary as the "Spouse of the Holy Spirit." In a dream of Brother Leo, Francis indicated to the friars that heaven could not be attained by hard penance but by trustful surrender to the loving mother of our Lord and Savior Jesus Christ.

Moreover, the mother church of St. Francis, the Portiuncula or St. Mary of the Angels, was revealed to him as a special "little portion" of Mary. Francis desired that this mother church of Mary be a place of pilgrimage—equal in significance (bearing an equal indulgence) to Rome and Jerusalem. When Francis died, he wanted to be laid naked on the floor of that little church—so that he would die in the arms of the Mother of God.

In the pseudo-Franciscan and pauperist mythology that in these days so many are applying to the new pope, imagination runs to a Church that would renounce power, structures, and wealth, and make itself purely spiritual. But it is not for this that the saint of Assisi lived. In the dream of Pope Innocent III painted by Giotto, Francis is not demolishing the Church but carrying it on his shoulders. And it is the Church of St. John Lateran, the cathedral of the bishop of Rome, at that time recently restored and decorated lavishly but made ugly by the sins of its men, who had to be purified. It was a few followers of Francis who fell into spiritualism and heresy.

PART THREE

In His Own Words

The Great Question of Human Life

What do I seek? Worldliness? Superficiality? Let us all think on this, it is a message for us all. These ashes pose the question to us: do I seek an encounter with Jesus that is going to fulfill me, that gives me the only happiness that cannot be lost? Or do I want a watered-down version of life? Am I mired in superficiality? —*Homily on Ash Wednesday, February 6, 2008*

If there is no Encounter with Jesus, life becomes inconsistent, loses its meaning. The Lord has given us a Eucharist—an encounter—every day, for us, for our families, for the entire Church, and our heart must learn to hold fast to this daily Eucharist, which is synthesized in the Sunday Mass, so that every day may be saved, blessed, converted into an offering, placed—as Jesus with his burden of love and the Cross is placed—in the hands of the Father. —*Homily on the Solemnity of Corpus Christi, June 17, 2006*

Wonder, Surprise
....

The beginning of every philosophy is wonder, and only wonder leads to knowledge.

. . . . . .

Pope Luciani once said that the drama of contemporary Christianity lies in the fact that it puts categories and norms in the place of wonder.

—*Presentation of the Spanish edition of Luigi Giussani's book* Il senso religioso [The Religious Sense], *October 16, 1998*

The Gospel tells us that Mary was surprised by what the angel said, that she stood there, maybe—I don't know—trembling. She was surprised. This is another prayer we could add to the litany: Our Lady, Virgin Surprised, pray for us! This Virgin who is open to the surprise, who opens her heart to the surprise, feels the impulse to serve. The surprise that opens her heart, the Spirit that surprises her, these inspire her to serve. —*Homily at the celebration of the papal elevation of the Cristífero Institute, Azul Cathedral, January 27, 2012*

Everything in our life, today just as in Jesus' time, begins with an encounter. An encounter with this Man, the carpenter of Nazareth, a man like all men and yet different. The first ones, John, Andrew, and Simon, felt a look that had pierced their innermost depths, read in their innermost being, and in them sprang forth a surprise, a wonder that instantly made them feel bound to Him, made them feel different. —*Presentation of the Spanish edition of Luigi Giussani's book* L'attrattiva Gesù *[The Attraction that is Jesus], April 27, 2001*

God

Where there is idolatry, God is negated, as is the dignity of man, made in the image of God. The new imperium of money shifts even the concept of work, which is how the dignity and creativity of man, the image of the creativity of God, is expressed. —*Interview in* 30 Giorni, *January 2002*

To worship is to say the name of God, and to say "life." To come face-to-face with the God of life in our daily lives is to worship him through life and through testimony. It is knowing that we have a faithful God who has remained at our side and who trusts in us as we do in Him. —*Letter to catechists, August 2002*

God makes an alliance with his people and with each of us so that we can make our way toward a promise, toward an encounter. This way is life. —*Homily on the Paschal Vigil, April 19, 2003*

The faith in God the Creator tells us that the history of humanity is not an unbounded void: it has a beginning, it has a direction. The God who created "heaven and earth" is the same one who has made a promise to His people, and His omnipotence is an assurance to us of the fruits of His Love. —*Message to the educational community, Metropolitan Cathedral, April 9, 2003*

We carry within us a promise and certainty of the faithfulness of God, but doubt is like a rock, the seal of corruption like a shackle, and often we yield to the temptation to remain paralyzed, without hope. Paralysis sickens the soul, robs us of memory, and takes away our joy. It makes us forget that we have been chosen, that we are bearers of a promise, that we are marked by a divine covenant. Paralysis deprives us of the surprise of the encounter, prevents us from receiving the "good news." —*Homily on the Paschal Vigil, April 19, 2003*

Even we, tonight, if we open our hearts, may contemplate the miracle of the light in the midst of our darknesses, the miracle of the strength of God in the midst of fragility, the miracle of supreme greatness in the midst of humbleness. —*Homily on Christmas Eve, 2003*

The presence of the Word of God made flesh transforms all humanity without negating it. It elevates us, it places us within the enormity of the Kingdom of God. —*Homily at the Journey for Life, Universidad Católica Argentina, March 25, 2004*

Lent is a time chosen for us to open ourselves and our fragility to the compassion of God our Father and to experience his tenderness. A time in which, in this newfound state of closeness, the Lord brings us closer also to our brothers, especially the smallest and most neglected. —*Letter to the priests and religious of the Archdiocese of Buenos Aires, February 11, 2004*

Human history, our history, the history of each one of us, of our families, of our communities, the concrete history that we construct day by day in our schools, is never "finished," never exhausted of possibility, but rather, is always open to new things, to that which, until the present moment, has not been considered. To what seemed impossible. Because this history forms part of a creation that has its roots in the Power and the Love of God. —*Message to the educational community, Metropolitan Cathedral, April 9, 2003*

Jesus Christ

If we look to Jesus, the Wisdom of God Incarnate, we realize that all difficulties become challenges, all challenges appeal to our hope, and all hope gives birth to the joy of knowing that we are the architects of something new. All of this, without a doubt, inspires us to continue to give the most of ourselves.

. . . . . .

Each encounter with Jesus changes our heart and emboldens us, makes us fearless, so that we defend what we have received, the truth that cannot be disputed.

. . . . . .

This is very clear: each encounter with Jesus makes us missionaries, because it founds us upon rock, not upon the sand of ideologies.

—*Message to the educational community, April 21, 2004*

And to encounter Jesus is an extraordinary thing, something that changes the path of our lives, that purifies our hearts, makes us extraordinary, magnanimous, with wide horizons that allow for the provision of all. —*Homily on the beginning of the academic year, April 22, 1999*

The key lies in Jesus, who feels our pain, draws near, touches pain and death, and transforms them into new life. He did not let hope be crushed by the mourning of the dead youth: "Do not mourn," he said to the mother and touched her pain. —Te Deum *Homily, May 25, 2000*

The church lives in memory of the Risen Christ. More than this; it has traveled on its historical path in the certainty that He who is Risen is He who was Crucified: the Lord whose coming we await is the same who pronounced the Beatitudes, who broke bread with the multitudes, who healed the sick, who forgave sinners, who sat at the table with the tax collectors. Remembering Jesus of Nazareth in the faith of the Lord Christ frees us to "do as he did," in memory of him. And in this the full dimension of memory is incorporated, because the story of Jesus is linked with the history of peoples and of all humanity, with their imperfect search for a fraternal banquet, for an enduring love. —*Message, March 29, 2000*

Holy Spirit

And this is what I ask of you today: that you be moved by the Holy Spirit to bring all of those around you into the Mystery of God. Make them enter into the Mystery; not by yourselves, but by the power of the Holy Spirit. Be the conduit of the Holy Spirit so that all in this society, our brothers and sisters, who have been baptized and anointed with the seal of the Spirit recognize that our journey is toward the Mystery of God. Fighting, we gain nothing. We must walk in the way of the Holy Spirit.

. . . . . .

The Anointing of the Holy Spirit is charity, gentleness, meekness, love. I ask this of you today: with gentleness, meekness, and love, let us guide our brothers and sisters so that the Holy Spirit may initiate them into the Mystery of God.

—*Homily at the Mass of the Renovación Carismática Católica, June 2, 2007*

Detached from the Holy Spirit, we run the risk of becoming disoriented in our understanding of faith and ultimately of Gnosticism. We also run the risk of not being "sent," but merely "out for our own"—disoriented in the hall of mirrors that is self-referentiality. By initiating us into the Mystery, the Holy Spirit saves us from a Gnostic church; by sending us on a mission it saves us from a self-referential one. —*Message to the fifth National Meeting of Priests, Villa Cura Brochero, September 11, 2008*

The Holy Spirit makes us adoptive children, liberates us from all bondage and, in true and mystical possession of us, gives us the gift of freedom and pronounces, from within, the invocation of our new allegiance: Father! —*Homily, Pilar, November 7, 2011*

Mary

Near the cross of Jesus, as we have heard, was his mother. She stood at the foot of the cross and continues to stand next to crosses of those who live with their own suffering. She is there, our Mother, wherever there is a cross, in the hearts of all of her children. The Gospels present this moment to us with few words but with a profound vision, a vision of the Virgin who looks at her son, a vision of the son who looks at her and gives her over as a Mother to all of us. Jesus gives his life and asks her to continue to keep watch over so many lives, our lives, that need protection. In the moment when Jesus speaks to his mother, when he is in the most complete isolation, the greatest abandonment, he has only her love and understanding gaze, and he commits her to the task of imparting to each one of us the motherly gaze of love and compassion in the most difficult moments of our own lives. —*Homily on the thirty-seventh Youth Pilgrimage to Luján, October 2, 2011*

Give us your hand, beloved Virgin, our Mother! Our hope is in your hands. You are she who tells us: "Do all as Jesus has said." May your injunction, tender yet demanding, spoken with the words of a mother, strengthen our hands, make them once again supple and tireless in work, fill them with the arduous joy of compassion. —*Homily on the Feast of San Cayetano, August 7, 2003*

Let us look to the Virgin Mary. She is the Mother and tells of all things, speaking as much to her Son as to us, her other children, her faithful people. To Jesus she speaks of our needs—that we have no wine, as in Cana. To us she speaks, telling us to do all as Jesus has said. In this way, by her lips which bless us, our union with Jesus grows and the Lord makes miracles out of the things of the earth: the water changes into wine, the bread multiplies and feeds all. —*Homily on the Solemnity of Corpus Christi, June 9, 2007*

Mother, teach us to listen. We are a people that needs to listen and that needs to be heard. Teach us to listen, we ask today, and she will teach us. Silent at the foot of the cross, she heard the essence of her life: "Behold your son . . . Behold your children!" and from that moment she began still more to hold the people of God in her care, to listen to them. She held all things that she had heard in her heart, and in this way brought us together to grow as a people, as Christians, as brothers and sisters. —*Homily on the twenty-fourth Youth Pilgrimage to Luján, October 5, 2008*

The Virgin Mother, who "keeps all things in her heart," teaches us the grace that comes with memory. Let us humbly ask to receive this grace. She speaks to us in our mother tongue, the tongue of our fathers, in which we babble as children. Let the love and tenderness of Mary, who whispers to us the words of God, never leave us. —*Message to the educational community, Buenos Aires, 1999*

Creation

All creation must enter into this authentic communion with God, which begins with the risen Christ. In other words, the end of God's will must be perfection, the genuine fulfillment of God's work through love: an end that is not an immediate or direct result of any action on our part, but is rather God's act of salvation, the final culmination of the work that He himself began and in which He enlisted us as free collaborators. —*Message, March 29, 2000*

Jesus wishes to reexperience, at the beginning of his new life, following his baptism, something akin to that which was in the beginning, and this act of Jesus, of living in peace with all of nature, in fruitful solitude of heart, and in temptation, shows us what he has come to do. He has come to restore, to re-create. In the saying of the Mass, during the liturgical year, we say a very beautiful thing: "God, who so masterfully created all things, and more masterfully re-created them." —*Homily to the Archdiocesan Meeting of Catechists, Balvanera, March 11, 2000*

In Christ, the centrality of man as a masterpiece of creation is fulfilled. By participating in this fullness we grasp more profoundly the mystery of man from the moment of his conception and the deontological natural order that guides his life. —*Homily at the Journey for Life, Universidad Católica Argentina, March 25, 2004*

The Pope has spoken of a transcendent dignity, expressed in a sort of "natural grammar," that emerges from the divine plan of creation. This transcendent character is perhaps the most characteristic thought of all of the religious conception of humanity. The true measure of who we are is not calculated simply in relation to the order of nature, biology, or even society, but rather in the mysterious link which, without sundering us from the Creation of which we form a part, unites us with the Creator that we may be not just a "part" of the world, but rather its culmination. Creation "is transcended" in humanity, the image and likeness of God. Because humanity is not only Adam; it is, above all, Christ, in whom all things were created, central in the divine plan.

· · · · · ·

Not only do we seek to recognize and live out a new eco-
logical consciousness, which supersedes all deterministic
reduction to the natural-biological, and a new humanistic
consciousness and oneness that stands in opposition to the
confusion of individual and economic opportunism, but as
the women and men that live on this earth, we dream of a
new world: a world that we probably will never see with our
own eyes in all its fullness, and yet we will it, we seek it, we
dream it.

—*Message to the educational community, April 18, 2007*

Humanity

· · · · · · · · · · · · · · · · ·

True growth in the consciousness of humanity must spring
from nothing less than the practice of dialogue and love. The
presence of dialogue and love means recognition of one another, the acceptance of our differences. —*Message to the educational community, April 10, 2002*

Our motivation, the reason why we care about education, is
hope—hope for a new humanity, hope in the possibility of
a new world. It is the hope that comes from Christian wisdom, which through the Risen Christ reveals to us the divine
nature to which we are called. —*Message to the educational community, April 21, 2004*

Church

The Church, as a fully "sanctified" reality, something capable of receiving and communicating—without error or omission, out of its own poverty and even with its sins—the full glory of God, is not a "complement" to or an "institutional aggregate" of Jesus Christ, but a full participation in his Incarnation, his Life, his Passion, death, and Resurrection. —*Catechesis at the forty-ninth International Eucharistic Congress, Quebec, June 18, 2008*

Unity in the Church is a blessing, a true blessing, but a blessing we must know how to receive, hoping dearly for it, making a place for it, making our hearts each time still more welcoming, stripping them of all worldly ties.

. . . . . .

On the other hand the temptation for the Church has been and will always be the same: to avoid the cross (cf. Mt. 16:22), compromise the truth, diminish the redemptive power of Christ's Cross to escape persecution. Oh wretched, lukewarm church that shuns and avoids the cross!

—*Homily at the ninety-second Plenary Assembly of the Pilar Episcopate, November 6, 2006*

The same devotion and reverence that we feel almost "spontaneously" in the presence of the Virgin and of the Eucharist we must cultivate and direct toward the Church. They must be the same, for, as we have seen, Mary and the Church are "recipients," wholly transformed by that which came to "dwell" within them. —*Catechesis at the forty-ninth International Eucharistic Congress, Quebec, June 18, 2008*

The Church puts us on a path, a path toward an encounter with Jesus Christ, the one path of constancy, the only one that will take us, somehow, toward an encounter with the Lord, the one who gives life meaning. —*Homily on Ash Wednesday, February 6, 2008*

Sacraments

The concern to encourage in every way the administration of baptism and the other sacraments involves the whole Church. If the Church follows its Lord, it comes out of itself, with courage and compassion: it doesn't remain locked in its own self. The Lord works a change in those who are faithful to Him, makes them look up away from themselves. That is the mission, that is witness.

. . . . . .

The sacraments are signs of the Lord. They are not performances or the conquests of priests or bishops.

. . . . . .

Nobody thinks that we don't need catechesis, preparing children for confirmation and communion. But we must always look at our people as they are, and see what is needed most. The sacraments are for the life of men and women as they are. Who maybe don't talk all that much, but their *sensus fidei* captures the reality of the sacraments with more clarity than that of many specialists.

—*Interview in* 30 Giorni, *November 8, 2009*

The Eucharist and the Church are covenant mysteries. With the word *covenant,* we want to bring out the ecclesial and nuptial dimensions of the gift of the Eucharist, through which the Lord wishes to give himself to all human beings. The Eucharist is living bread given for the life of the world and blood poured out for the sins of all human beings.

. . . . . .

The Church's sacraments allow us to share fully in the life the Lord came to bring us.

—*Catechesis at the International Eucharistic Congress, Quebec, June 18, 2008*

The Eucharist

If the Church is born and journeys for the life of the world, the most important moment for its task is therefore the institution of the Eucharist. Its foundation sums up the entirety of the Easter Triduum. All is contained and summed up in the Eucharist.

. . . . . .

Jesus Christ has entrusted the Church with the permanent actualization of the Easter mystery. With this gift, he instituted a mysterious oneness in time between the Easter Triduum and the Church's life through the centuries. Each time we celebrate the sacred mystery, the wellsprings of the Church are anticipated and summed up in the Eucharist. It is through this gift that the Lord brings about that mysterious oneness in time between himself and the centuries that pass.

. . . . . .

A phrase of the *Instrumentum Laboris* says that "we are to see if the law of prayer corresponds to the law of faith. We are to consider what the People of God believes and how the People of God lives, so that the Eucharist can become more and more the source and summit of the life and mission of . . . the Church." A very rich intuition that goes looking for Christ in his most humble beneficiaries and witnesses: in the holy faithful People of God, the people that, in their entirety, are infallible *in credendo*.

—*Catechesis at the International Eucharistic Congress, Quebec, June 18, 2008*

Our faithful people have the true "Eucharistic attitude" of giving thanks and of praise. Remembering Mary, they are grateful for being remembered by her, and this memorial of love is truly Eucharistic. In this respect I repeat what John Paul II affirmed in *Ecclesia de Eucharistia* number 58: "The Eucharist has been given to us so that our life, like that of Mary, can become completely a Magnificat. —*Intervention in the eleventh Ordinary General Assembly of the Synod of Bishops, October 2–23, 2005*

Freedom

The transcendent dignity of an individual implies a transcendence with respect to one's own ego, as well as the necessary openness toward the *other*. The Christian concept of "human being" has little to do with the entrenched postmodern view of the individual as a uniquely social agent. Freedom is not an end in itself, a black hole unconstrained by external forces, but it is rather that from which arises a most robust way of life of the individual and the entirety of mankind.

. . . . . .

Such a definition of "negative" freedom presents as the only option if our point of origin rests on the absolutism of the individual; it is not the sole choice if we take into account that the entire human race is intimately tied to its likeness, and its community. In effect, if it is true that the word, a uniquely human trait, is not borne exclusively from our inner selves, but instead is amassed through the words that have been transmitted to us and have made us who we are (the "native language," our language and our mother); if it is true that outside of history and community, there is no humanity (because nobody is "self-created," contrary to what the sensationalist ideologies of depredation and competition have prescribed); if our speech is only ever a response to the voice that first speaks to us (and, ultimately, to the voice that gives us being), what other meaning can freedom have than opening oneself to the possibility of being one with others? What use is my freedom if I do not have even the companionship of a barking dog? Why do I want to create a world in which I am alone in a prison of luxury?

. . . . . .

From this point of view, freedom does not "end," but rather "begins" where the freedom of all begins.

. . . . . .

Freedom is fully, "maturely" realized when it is responsible. Thus it becomes the nexus of the three facets of time [possibly referring to the Neoplatonic hypothesis of different strata of time]. A freedom that is cognizant of what has come to pass and what has not, from the here-and-now looking back to the past, takes ownership of itself in every present moment and is responsible for the consequences, from the present to the future. This is a mature freedom.

—*Message to the educational community of Buenos Aires, April 6, 2005*

Morality

Christian morality is not a titanic effort of the will, the effort of someone who decides to be consistent and succeeds, a solitary challenge in the face of the world. No. Christian morality is simply a response. It is the heartfelt response to a surprising, unforeseeable, "unjust" mercy. . . . The surprising, unforeseeable, "unjust" mercy, using purely human criteria, of one who knows me, knows my betrayals and loves me just the same, appreciates me, embraces me, calls me again, hopes in me, and expects from me. This is why the Christian conception of morality is a revolution; it is not a never falling down but an always getting up again. —*Buenos Aires, 2001*

Today, amidst the conflict, this community shows us that the views of those who profess to distill reality into abstractions need not be accepted, that neither intellectuals without talent nor ethicists without compassion serve us well. Instead, we must appeal to the source of our dignity as a people, to our wisdom as individuals and as a whole. This is a true revolution; not a revolution against a system, but an interior one, based on memory and tenderness; a revolution founded on the memory of our greatest and most heroic actions, on the memory of the simple and profound actions that constitute the life of the family. —Te Deum *Homily at the 189th anniversary of the May Revolution*

The Defense of Life

··

How wonderful it is to protect life, to let life grow, to give life like Jesus, and to give it abundantly, to not permit even one of the smallest to be lost.

· · · · · ·

We cannot announce anything other than life, and from the beginning to the end. We must all care for life, cherish life, tenderness, warmth. That is what we are called to today, and that's beautiful.

· · · · · ·

We must fight for life, guard life, that there does not have to be even one person who does not have the right to be born, that there does not have to be one person who does not have the right to proper nutrition, that there does not have to be one person who does not have the right to go to school.

· · · · · ·

To protect life from its beginning to its end, how simple a thing, how beautiful.

—*Homily, Sanctuary of San Ramón Nonato, August 31, 2009*

Children

. . . .

The children of today run the risk, because of poor nutrition, because of poor or insufficient education, of not being able to fully integrate themselves into society. A "caste of have-nots" is being created. A boy who does not receive sufficient protein in the first years of his life will enter the ranks of the mentally handicapped. This is an issue that must be dealt with—the children of today, who have been so treacherously handicapped and shunned. When we read in the news about boats filled with child slaves we tear at our clothes with shame, but this is not something happening elsewhere; it happens whenever there is no policy centered on the protection of our youth as human beings. I see this as a great issue of our time. —*Remarks at the fourth Pastoral and Social Journey, Almagro, June 30, 2001*

Youth

. . . .

To be young is to entertain oneself by looking out at the horizon, and to not keep oneself locked up. Youth is maturation toward a triumphant victory; that is to say, learning how to fight, learning how to work, learning how to see the world with eyes wide open. To be young is to contain multitudes.

. . . . . .

You young ones are being called to great things, to the service of all in need, to carry the torch of our people, to form a family and impart the values of our community. Do not let yourselves be deceived, do not let yourselves become numb, for not all that glitters is gold, often it is merely colored glass.

—*Homily, Parish of Santa Inés, Virgin Martyr, January 21, 2004*

Justice

In the most poor, and in all those who work or are wearily seeking work, who do not allow themselves to be swept away by the destructive marginalization nor by the temptation of organized violence, perseveres, silently and with the devotion that is conferred by faith, an ardent love of their land. Through their devotion and service they have tasted the cup of balm and hope. In them is manifested the great cultural and moral reserve of our people. They are those who listen to the word, who do without the public applause [*los aplausos rituales*, referring possibly to the complex system of ritual applause for public representatives used in ancient Rome], those who come to reflect the true word and understand that it is spoken for them. —Te Deum *Homily, Metropolitan Cathedral, May 25, 2001*

Our coexistence, our joint creation of the common good, is imperative—a common good in which special interests are abrogated so that stakes are held equally and rewards dispensed justly, in which society is at peace. This is not to propose merely a new administrative or technical order, but rather to advance a conviction that must be expressed constantly through actions, through personal relations, as a hallmark, in which our will to turn away from our mania for the ever-greater accrual of riches, to turn toward hope, toward a new culture of closeness and dialogue, is given voice. In this new culture, the privileged are no longer beyond reproach, and exploitation and abuse are no longer the habits of survival. —Te Deum *Homily, May 25, 2000*

Modernity

In saying that the crisis is global, then, we bring under our scrutiny the great precepts of our culture, the most rooted beliefs, the criteria by which we hold things to be "good" or "bad" ("positive" or "negative"), "desirable" or "disposable." What is in crisis is an entire system of grasping reality and ourselves. —*Message given on March 29, 2000*

Sometimes we think of the values and traditions, even of our own culture, as a kind of ancient and inalterable jewel, something that remains in a space and time apart, not polluted by the comings and goings of concrete history. Let me say that this view leads one only to the museum, and eventually, to sectarianism. Christians have suffered for too long the sterile polemics of traditionalists and progressivists to allow ourselves to fall once again into attitudes of this nature. —*Message to the educational community, April 10, 2002*

Culture

Recovering our memory signifies, to the contrary, reflecting on the blossoming of a soul that resists oppression. In our community there are popular artistic meetings where feeling and humanity are nurtured; there is a return to the faith and to the spiritual journey in the face of the breakdown of materialism, scientism, and ideology; the spontaneous coming together of the community is an active force in the pursuit of the common good. These popular approaches, *emerging out of our cultural reserve*, transcend sectarianism, partisanship, and petty conflict. —Te Deum *Homily, Metropolitan Cathedral, May 25, 2001*

As individuals, we have a complex relationship to the world in which we live, precisely because of our double condition as children of the earth and children of God. We are part of the natural world; we are subject to the same physical, chemical, and biological dynamics as all other beings that share in the world with us. Though it has become trivialized to say, and is so often misunderstood, we are a piece of the whole, an element of the magnificent equilibrium of Creation. The earth is our home. The earth is our body. We, too, are the earth. Nevertheless, in our modern civilization, we are out of harmony with the world. Nature has become a mere quarry, to be mined in the furthering of economic dominion and exploitation. And so our home, our body, a piece of us, is degraded. Modern civilization contains within itself this dimension, the dimension of degradation. Why is this? In terms of what we have been discussing, this rupture (which, without a doubt, will cost us and is already causing us great suffering, even putting a question mark on our very survival), this rupture, I would say, can be understood as a sort of "de-natured transcendence," as if man's transcendence of nature and the world implies a separation. Before we came into contact with nature, we encountered nature, and in it we saw reflected our transcendence, our humanity. And thus it was for us. But transcendence of nature does not mean that we may wantonly break away from its dynamics. Our freedom and capacity to investigate, comprehend, and modify the world in which we live does not mean that "anything goes." We have not followed its "laws," nor will our ignorance be without serious consequences. This applies as well to the intrinsic laws that govern our own being in the world; as humanity, we are able to lift our heads above the natural determinisms . . . but so that we may see their richness and meaning, and free them from their limitations, not so that we may ignore them; so that we may even the odds, not trample the results of hundreds of thousands of years of fine calibration. This is the role of science and technology, which cannot take place decoupled from the deep currents of life; free, yes, but not alienated from the natural world that has been given to us. Science and technology exist in the creative dimension: from the earliest primordial ignorance, through intelligence and work, they bring culture into being. But if the laws that the natural world holds within itself are not respected, then human activity becomes destructive, chaos-producing, a new form of ignorance, a new chaos capable of the destruction of the world and of humanity. —*Message to the educational community, April 18, 2007*

Today we live in a culture of abundance, where everything that is not functional is disposable, be it young or old. This culture is a "new image" that is expressed in the idea of a historical progress, without roots and in "demographic terrorism." [Bergoglio has denounced "demographic terrorism" as "the right of a mother to kill her children or vice versa."] —*Buenos Aires, October 2, 2007*

Politics and Peace

The political vocation is truly a vocation—here I am twisting the word, but only to show its nobility—a vocation that is almost sacred, because it is what aids us in the development of the common good, of creativity and of prosperity. We will do well to remember the phrase "politics is not a tool for generating crisis." There are times when we must put out the fire, but the job description is not that of a firefighter. Politics serves to promote creation and prosperity. —*Remarks at the fourth Pastoral and Social Journey, Almagro, June 30, 2001*

Power is but a service. Power only makes sense if it is in the service of the common good. —Te Deum *Homily, Metropolitan Cathedral, May 25, 2001*

The idea of a "politics of transversality" has been mentioned (what has been referred to as a "politics of transversality"). It has been urged that this is the way, a way not of atomization nor of "hunting preserves." I would say that there is no transversality without dialogue. If there is no debate of the ideas surrounding the search for the common good, then we will be rendered paralyzed This is a good occasion on which to realign our political action and reorient ourselves toward a path of innovation and initiative. —*Remarks at the fourth Pastoral and Social Journey, Almagro, June 30, 2001*

Every economic, political, social, or religious project involves the inclusion or exclusion of the wounded lying on the side of the road. Each day, each of us faces the choice of being a good Samaritan or an indifferent bystander. —*Homily on the Good Samaritan, May 2003*

As all is lost in war, all is won in peace. In peace, we gain dignity and respect, because peace is the fruit of justice. Justice comes to us through the image of God we hold in our hearts. As all is won in peace, all is lost in war. These words, which are not my own, but are those of a great Pope, who defended and carried forth the declaration of *Nostra aetate*, come as his request to us: a request that we keep these words in our heart and in our prayers, so that they may accompany us in our lives. —*Interfaith address for peace in the Gaza Strip, Cathedral of Buenos Aires, November 22, 2012*

Religion

Far from disappearing, religion is in fact acquiring new significance in our modern world. What is more, it has once more begun to encapsulate those enigmatic aspects which, for a time, had seemingly evaporated. Ideas of mysticism that had previously been circumscribed as being those of "primitive" or "traditional" cultures are once again gaining popularity. At the same time, certain fundamentalist views are becoming more radicalized, as with Islam, so with Christianity and Judaism. —*Message, March 29, 2000*

The Future

Memory of our roots, courage in the face of the unknown, capturing the reality of the present moment—a people that cannot make sense of the reality they are living becomes atomized, fragmented, because self-interest is then privileged above the common good and the common interest, and people are atomized in this multiplicity of self-interests that are born from a flawed analysis of the reality that they are living.
—*Remarks, June 28, 2003*

Education is an investment in the future, a future that is governed by hope. —*Message to the educational community, April 18, 2007*

Time

Personal maturity can be understood as the capacity to use one's freedom in a way that is "sensible" and "prudent." The dialogue and teaching surrounding the words *sense* and *prudence* have much to do with maturity. Because in order to reach this state of working and living in a "sensible" way, a person must have experienced many things, made many choices, responded many times to the challenges of life. It is obvious that "sense" comes with time. Above all, then, as it is in the biological and psychological fields, to speak of maturity is to speak of time.

· · · · · ·

The Gospel offers us a beautiful image of the Holy Family "taking its time," watching Jesus becoming a man, "growing in wisdom, in stature, and in grace before God and men" (Lk 23–52). It is this man who, in time, God made the principal focus of his plan of salvation. The hope of his people is concentrated and symbolized in that hope of Mary and Joseph for the child who "is taking his time," developing his identity and his mission, and who later as a man, waits still in his public life for the critical moment, "the coming of his hour."

—*Message to the educational community, Buenos Aires, April 6, 2005*

Suffering

Today, in this city, we wish for the call, the question of God, to be heard: Where is your brother? We wish for this question to resound in all the neighborhoods of this city, in our hearts, and, above all, in the hearts of all modern-day "Cains." Perhaps someone will ask: "What brother?" Your brother enslaved! He whom you are killing day by day in the sweatshops, in the net of prostitution, in the huts of the children who are used for begging, for drug-distribution "campaigns," for rape and prostitution! Your brother who has to work almost in secret as a *cartonero* [pasteboard maker] because he has still not been naturalized! Where is your brother? And faced with this question we can do as the priest who passed by the wounded man, and distract ourselves; as the Levite, and look the other way, for "it is not my concern, but another's." But it is the concern of all of us! For entrenched within this city is a system, a system of what was described so aptly by an official a few days ago as "that *mafioso* and aberrant crime," of human trafficking.

And where is your brother? You who are standing by, who distract yourselves, who leave no room in your heart even for the question to enter, who say, "It is not my concern"—who is not your concern? The slave? The ones who in this city suffer the forms of bondage that I have mentioned, because this is an "open city," and everybody, including those who wish to enslave and rape, may enter? When a city capitulates it declares itself an "open city" and can be despoiled; here they are despoiling the lives of our youth! The lives of our laborers! The lives of our families! These traffickers . . . no, let us not curse them, but rather pray that they, too, will hear the voice of God: Where is your brother?

To you, trafficker, today we say this: Why do such things? You are bringing yourself nothing; only hands heavy with blood from the evil that you have done. And speaking of blood, that is what you will receive out there, your blood from a competitor's bullet. That is how the *mafias* are. Where is your brother, trafficker? He is your brother! He is your flesh! Let us recognize that this flesh in bondage is our flesh, the same flesh assumed by the Son of God. —*Homily at the fifth Mass for the Victims of Human Trafficking, Buenos Aires*

Loneliness

It is a time for the adoration of God, for being more supportive, more honest, more compassionate, more engaged with those who weep and suffer, with those who live in solitude and who feel excluded. It is a time of grace, a time to change our attitudes and to commit ourselves to tireless work so that the day may come when no one person on this earth must live year-round the austere and abstinent life of Lent. —*Message on Ash Wednesday, February 6, 2008*

Each and every one of us must come together as Samaritan neighbors, as we are all just as sinful as the Samaritan; however, we are summoned by God to come nearer, to reach out and touch the pain and misery, injustice, and the hidden wounds and loneliness of our elders, to come as neighbors and touch the wounds of our brothers, for they are the wounds of Jesus Christ. —*Homily, Parish of San Ildefonso, July 15, 2001*

Sin

Little by little we grow accustomed to hearing and witnessing, by all modern means of communication, the dark chronicle of contemporary society, presented with an almost perverse relish. We grow accustomed even to touching and feeling it in our surroundings, in our very flesh. The drama is in the street, in the community, in our homes; how could it not be also in our hearts? We live alongside the violence that kills, that destroys families, that fuels wars and conflicts in so many countries of the world. We live with envy, hatred, slander, triviality in our hearts. We are constantly faced with the suffering of the innocent and the peaceful; the contempt for the rights of the most fragile individuals and communities is never far removed from us; the rule of money with its demonic effects—drugs, corruption, human trafficking even of children—together with moral and material misery, is the currency of the day. The destruction of the dignity of labor, displacement, and the lack of a future also join in this symphony. Nor are our errors and sins as a church an exception. The most personal selfishness—ever rationalized, yet no smaller, the lack of ethical values within society, which, like a cancer, metastasizes within families and within the communities of our neighborhoods, towns, and cities—all of these speak to our limitations, our weaknesses, and our incapacity to transform this innumerable list of destructive realities. . . .

The snare of powerlessness makes us wonder: Does it make sense to try to change all of this? Can anything be done in the face of this situation? Is it worthwhile to try, as long as the world continues this absurd carnivalesque masquerade, disguising everything for a bit longer? Yet without fail, the mask falls, the truth is unveiled, and although to many it may sound anachronistic to say, sin once again rears its head; it is, once again, sin that wounds our flesh with all its destructive force, twisting the destinies of the world and of history. —*Lenten Message, 2013*

Death

....

Life is beautiful, but life is onerous. Always. The other day
a father who had just had his first child was telling me that
both he and his wife are sleeping just two hours every night
because this creature is constantly wailing! Life is beautiful,
but onerous, because it requires a sacrifice, a sacrifice from
me. When one sees these men and women with their termi-
nally ill parents, who spend evenings sitting, holding their
hands so that they can feel the love, and who go to work the
next day and do it all over again . . . it is onerous, but that is
life. One cannot share in the culture of life, in proclaiming
life, if life is not as it has been described in the Psalms: in
the presence of God. —*Homily, Sanctuary of San Ramón Nonato,
August 31, 2009*

Today, in solidarity more than ever before, we are brothers
and sisters in pain and as brothers and sisters let us look
toward the sky. . . . Father, why? And let each one of us
open our hearts. And let us continue to ask "Why?" I cannot provide you with the answer, nor can any bishop, nor
the Pope, but He can give you solace. Only He may come
to us and, in the harmony of his Fatherly presence, make
us feel that the mystery of life and death has meaning even
when it is brought about by irresponsible hands. —*Homily at
the Mass commemorating the Once rail tragedy, Metropolitan Cathedral,
March 23, 2012*

The Heart

In this season of Lent, we hear the voice of true hope crying out in the wilderness, telling us "Yes! It is possible to wash away your mask and unveil your true faces, to not conceal yourselves behind plastic smiles as if you were impervious. Yes, it is possible for everything to be distinctly new, because God continues to be 'rich in kindness and compassion, always ready to forgive,' and inspires us to begin again and again." Today we are invited once more to undertake a paschal journey toward life, a journey marked by the cross and renunciation, which although uncomfortable will be a fruitful one. We are invited to come face-to-face with the deficiencies within ourselves, our communities, and our churches, to make a change in the right direction, to convert ourselves once more.

On this day, we do well to remember the strong words of the prophet Joel, which ring out as a challenge to us: *Rend your heart and not your garments. Give yourselves unto the Lord your God.* It is an invitation and a challenge to all; none are exempt, none excluded.

Rend your heart and not the garments of superficial penitence which makes no promise of a better future.

Rend your heart and not your garments of perfunctory abstinence and mechanical formality, a formality that continues to keep us complacent.

Rend your heart and not the garments of empty and egocentric prayer, which does not approach the essence of one's own life nor allow it to be touched by God.

Rend your hearts, that we may say, together with the Psalmist, "We have sinned." "The wound of the soul is sin. Oh, wounded soul, know your healer! Show him the wounds of your errors. Knowing that from him no secret is hidden, let him feel the lamentation of your heart. Move him to compassion through your tears, through your insistence; implore him! So that he hears your sighs, so that your pain reaches him, so that at last he may reply: The Lord has forgiven your sins" (St. Gregory the Great). This is the reality of the human condition. This is the truth that brings us closer to true reconciliation—with God and with one another. It is not about the diminishment of our self-esteem, but rather a matter of penetrating the depths of our hearts and becoming aware of the mystery of pain and suffering that has bound us through ages of ages.

Rend your hearts so that through our wounds we can truly see ourselves.

Rend your hearts, open your hearts, for only through a heart that has been torn open can the compassionate love of the Father, who loves and heals us, enter.

Rend your hearts, says the prophet, and Paul requests, almost begs, of us: "Let yourselves be reconciled with God." Changing our way of life is a sign, a legacy of a heart that has been torn open and reconciled to a transcendent love. . . .

This is the invitation, in the face of so many wounds that hurt us, tempt us to become desensitized, deadened, and scarred: *Rend your hearts* to experience in silent and serene reflection the gentle tenderness of God.

Rend your hearts to feel the echo of so many lives rent and torn apart, so that we are not left sluggish with indifference.

Rend your hearts to love in the way that we are loved, comfort in the way that we are comforted, and share what has been shared with us.

The liturgical season that the Church begins today is not only for us, but for the transformation of our community, of our family, of our Church, of our country, of the entire world. Forty days for us to strive toward the holiness of God, to become collaborators in receiving His grace and in reconstructing our shared human life so that we all may experience the salvation that Christ won for us through his death and resurrection. —*Lenten Message, 2013*

Let us open our hearts wide! Let each of us open our heart, and gazing upon the Virgin, feel the presence of Jesus in the Eucharist that has silently accompanied mankind for two thousand years. Let us open the hearts of our families, to each their own, feeling the heartbeat of our parents and siblings, of our spouses and young ones, of our children and grandparents, alike. Let us open our hearts as the faithful people of God on this pilgrimage in Argentina under the mantle of the Virgin Mary of Itati. . . . Let us open our hearts and be reunited with our God, the Father! —*Homily at the National Eucharistic Congress, September 2, 2004*

Prayer

Juan Diego was a simple man. He knew the catechism and the prayers. Nothing more. —*Homily on the Feast of Our Lady of Guadalupe, December 12, 2011*

Today, in the house of our Mother, we come to make a request: we request that she teach us to work for justice. Do you know to whom it occurred to make this request? To you yourselves, all of you. Indeed, in the prayers that are written by visitors to Luján, one appeared over and over, the prayer which today is our mantra: "Mother, teach us to work for justice." It is a mantra and prayer that lives in the hearts of all of the pilgrims of the Virgin. —*Homily on the thirty-eighth Youth Pilgrimage to Luján*

Faith

In this season of Lent, we return, through conversion, to the roots of faith, to contemplate the immeasurable gift of Redemption, and we realize that all that has been given to us has been given freely, as an act of our God.

. . . . . .

There is no true faith that is not manifested in love, and love is not Christian if it is not generous and tangible. An exceptionally generous love is a sign and an invitation to faith. When we take care of the needs of our brothers and sisters, as did the Good Samaritan, we are announcing the Kingdom and bringing it into existence.

—*Letter for the beginning of Lent, February 22, 2012*

The experience of Faith places us in the Experience of the Spirit, marked by the capacity to put ourselves on the right path. . . . There is nothing more contradictory to the Spirit than to enclose and idle oneself. When we do not pass through the doors of Faith, those doors close to us, the Church is barred to us, the heart withdraws, and fear and evil spirits sour the Good News. When the Chrism of Faith has dried up and become rancid the evangelist can no longer impart his news because he has lost his fragrance, having too often become the cause of scandal and the distancing of many. —*Letter to catechists, August 21, 2012*

Hope

In order to cross the threshold of faith, one must have the heart of a child who, believing still in the impossible, can live in hope and anticipation; a child, who alone can transform and give meaning to history. —*Opening remarks for the Year of Faith, Buenos Aires, November 2012*

When God chose his people, He made a covenant with them and sowed hope in their hearts. He did not deal in illusions, but hope. —*Audiovisual production of the Centro Televisivo Arquidiocesano, Buenos Aires, December 23, 2011*

Love
········

The Gospel of Matthew (25:31) presents us with the "test" that the Lord gives to his own at the end of time: if you have fed the hungry, if you have given a drink to those who thirst, if you have received the traveler into your home . . . In the disciples who fulfilled these tasks we observe the miracle of the dynamic presence of God, the achievement of communion: Christ himself identifies with the one who is offered love—symbolically reversing the roles, as it is he who offers, gives, transforms, and creates a new reality through his love.
—*Message for the start of the academic year, March 28, 2001*

The reality we are faced with is complicated and disconcerting, but as Christians, we must live in this reality as disciples of the Master. We cannot be lifeless and impartial observers, but, instead, men and women passionate about the King, eager to imbue all structures in society with a Life and Love we have come to know. This Love makes us live in abundance, just as the Pope has told us in his inaugural message: "[It is] the best thing that has come to pass in our lives," that which we have to offer to the world and with which we counter the culture of death with the Christian culture of life and solidarity. Because of this, we cannot conceive of reality in any other terms than those of the mission. —*Letter to catechists, August 21, 2008*

Holiness
. . . .

By defending her identity and infallibility, the Church defends the conduit through which the gift of life to the world
passes—the gift of the life of the world to God. What the
Church is defending when she defends her integrity is her
own identity. This gift, the most beautiful expression of
which is the Eucharist, is not a gift among others but the
most intimate and complete self-giving of the Trinity given
for the life of the world, a gift made by the Son who offers
himself to the Father. —*Catechesis at the International Eucharistic
Congress, Quebec, June 18, 2008*

Eternal Life
. . . .

The cross is only meaningful for those of us who believe in
eternal life. For the one who does not believe in eternal life
but instead believes that all that exists is created here and
ends here, and lives as though this were true, for him, the
cross bears no meaning, nor does he understand it, that it is
not a decoration to be hung as the latest fashion—and not
some other thing altogether!—nor does he understand it as
the triumph of God's salvation of us all.

. . . . . .

And gazing upon the cross and seeing clearly the vision of
eternal life, and gazing upon the cross and declaiming that
"No! These idols are not undeniable and they will perish
with me. These idols do not have meaning which transcends

into the afterlife," let us ask ourselves if we have surrendered ourselves to the search for God's love.

—Homily at the twentieth Exposición del Libro Católico, September 14, 2008

True Joy

Listen well to this, so that there may be a celebration in each of your hearts: we must give joy to others, we must make others joyful, so that they arrive at the Feast of Jesus with open hearts. And this can be done. Each of us can make our companions, our brothers and sisters, our neighbors, our families, our friends, all of them, joyful. Each one of you, each boy and girl, can bring joy to your friends and your families, each one of you can do good unto others.

To you, girls and boys, I say just this: Walk in the light, do not be seduced by the merchants of darkness; open your hearts to the light, even if it costs you. Do not be chained by what seem to be the promises of liberty but are in fact those of oppression; the promises of fatuous joy, of darkness. Continue forward. The world is yours. Live within it in the light. And live in it with joy, because he who walks in the light has a joyful heart. This is what I wish for all of you. *—Homily at the Archdiocesan Mass for Children, Parque Roca, October 24, 2009*

EPILOGUE

During his first Holy Week as leader to 1.2 billion Catholics around the world, Pope Francis raised eyebrows when he decided to celebrate Holy Thursday Mass—the Mass of the Lord's Supper, called in Latin *"in coena Domini"*—in a Roman prison for youthful offenders called Casal del Marmo instead of in a larger church. And when he celebrated the Mass, he chose to go beyond the traditional instructions for the ceremony of foot washing, which commemorates Christ's washing of the feet of the twelve apostles.

Traditionally, and according to current Church regulations, the priest or bishop celebrating this Mass washes only the feet of men, not women, as the ceremony is seen as a commemoration of the institution of the sacrament of Holy Orders. But Francis chose to wash the feet of two women, one of whom was not a Catholic at all but a Muslim. This caused general surprise, and considerable debate about what the pope intended by this decision.

The pope himself did not explain himself at length. In fact, his homily for the occasion was very brief. But he gave some insight into his thinking in the homily he delivered that morning at the Holy Thursday Chrism Mass in St. Peter's Basilica. And, on March 30, the *Osservatore Romano* revealed that the text of this homily, "with the exception of some additions," was identical to the text of a homily Bergoglio had prepared before he was elected pope and which was read at the March 28 Chrism Mass celebrated in the cathedral of Buenos Aires. The text hints at his reasoning for the decision he made:

> A good priest can be recognized by the way his people are anointed: this is a clear proof. . . . When our people are anointed with the oil of gladness, it is obvious: for example, when they leave Mass looking as if they have heard good news. . . . People thank us because they feel that we have prayed over the realities of their everyday lives, their troubles, their joys, their burdens, and their hopes. And when they feel that the fragrance of the Anointed One, of Christ, has come to them through us, they feel encouraged to entrust to us everything they want to bring before the Lord. . . . When we have this relationship with God and with his people, and grace passes through us, then we are priests, mediators between God and men.

Pope Francis was clearly saying that he wished the Church to preach about the "everyday lives" of people, "their troubles, their joys." He was saying that he wanted the Church to go out toward the people, to reach them where they were.

> We need to "go out," then, in order to experience our own anointing, its power and its redemptive efficacy: to the 'outskirts' where there is suffering, bloodshed, blindness that longs for sight, and prisoners in thrall

to many evil masters. It is not in soul-searching or
constant introspection that we encounter the Lord:
self-help courses can be useful in life, but to live our
priestly life going from one course to another, from
one method to another, leads us to become Pelagians
and to minimize the power of grace, which comes
alive and flourishes to the extent that we, in faith,
go out and give ourselves and the Gospel to others,
giving what little ointment we have to those who
have nothing, nothing at all.

In his very brief homily that evening for the young
people at the prison, Pope Francis made quite clear that he
was not trying to imply that he wished to ordain women
to the priesthood—that was not on his mind. Rather, he
was trying to give an example of love through service, an
example he hoped the young people would see and follow.

Pope Francis preached to the young people whose feet he
washed and kissed.

Help one another. This is what Jesus teaches us, and
this what I am doing, and doing with all my heart,
because it is my duty. As a priest and a bishop, I
must be at your service. But it is a duty which comes
from my heart: I love it. I love this and I love to do
it because that is what the Lord has taught me to
do. But you too, help one another: help one another
always. One another. In this way, by helping one
another, we will do some good.

He concluded:

Now we will perform this ceremony of washing
feet, and let us think, let each one of us think: "Am
I really willing, willing to serve, to help others?"
Let us think about this, just this. And let us think
that this sign is a caress of Jesus, which Jesus gives,
because this is the real reason why Jesus came: to
serve, to help us.

This profound appeal to the hearts and souls of these
young people was the pope's way of trying to open them
up to a transformation of their lives, to an encounter with
Christ. There was a risk in his action to wash the feet of
the young women. Francis was apparently going against a
Church liturgical teaching by doing so. But Francis took
the risk.

In his homily for the Easter Vigil, just before midnight
on Holy Saturday, March 30, in a St. Peter's Basilica that had
been filled with the light of the thousands of candles lit from
the one Paschal candle ignited by Pope Francis, the final passage was as follows:

Let the risen Jesus enter your life, welcome him
as a friend, with trust: he is life! If up till now
you have kept him at a distance, step forward. He
will receive you with open arms. If you have been
indifferent, take a risk: you won't be disappointed.
If following him seems difficult, don't be afraid,
trust him, be confident that he is close to you, he
is with you and he will give you the peace you are
looking for and the strength to live as he would
have you do.

In this way, Pope Francis continued on his mission, even if it required taking some risks, to bring to a suffering world the light of the Risen Christ.

On Easter Sunday, the first Easter Sunday of his pontificate, the pope preached at the end of Mass from the same balcony where he had spoken the first words of his pontificate on the night of March 13.

"Dear brothers and sisters in Rome and throughout the world, Happy Easter! Happy Easter!" Francis said.

> What a joy it is for me to announce this message: Christ is risen!
>
> I would like it to go out to every house and every family, especially where the suffering is greatest, in hospitals, in prisons.
>
> Most of all, I would like it to enter every heart, for it is there that God wants to sow this Good News: Jesus is risen, there is hope for you, you are no longer in the power of sin, of evil! Love has triumphed, mercy has been victorious! The mercy of God always triumphs!
>
> We too, like the women who were Jesus' disciples, who went to the tomb and found it empty, may wonder what this event means (cf. Lk 24:4).
>
> What does it mean that Jesus is risen? It means that the love of God is stronger than evil and death itself; it means that the love of God can transform our lives and let those desert places in our hearts bloom. The love of God can do this!
>
> This same love for which the Son of God became man and followed the way of humility

and self-giving to the very end, down to hell—to the
abyss of separation from God—this same merciful
love has flooded with light the dead body of Jesus,
has transfigured it, has made it pass into eternal life.

Jesus did not return to his former life, to earthly
life, but entered into the glorious life of God and
he entered there with our humanity, opening us to a
future of hope.

This is what Easter is: it is the exodus, the passage
of human beings from slavery to sin and evil to the
freedom of love and goodness. Because God is life,
life alone, and we are his glory: the living man (cf.
Irenaeus, *Adversus Haereses*, 4, 20, 5–7).

We are his glory.

These were the words that Francis spoke, and they sum
up his most profound, Christ-centered spirituality. Francis
believes that living men and women are God's glory, that
God is glorified when men and women live, and live fully.
And when they live fully, they love, they work for justice, and
they build a world where children are not harmed, where the
feet of prisoners are washed, where the face of God, and the
will of God, can be seen in the faces of men and women—in
the face of a man like Pope Francis, who asks of us something very simple:

"Pray for me."

APPENDIX

Cardinal Bergoglio's Last Words
Before His Election

On March 26, the "last words" spoken by Cardinal Bergoglio to his fellow cardinals before his election as pope were made public (with the new pope's permission) on a Church website in Havana, Cuba.

It is widely believed that when the other cardinals heard these thoughtful words during their meetings on March 9, just four days before the election of Pope Francis on March 13, their support for Bergoglio's candidacy grew and solidified.

The preconclave remarks were made public by the cardinal of Havana, Jaime Lucas Ortega y Alamino, the Italian Vatican journalist Sandro Magister reported on March 27.

Cardinal Ortega was present on March 9 in Rome when Bergoglio spoke. After hearing Bergoglio's words, he approached Bergoglio to ask if he could have a written text to keep. Bergoglio said he did not have a written text. However, the next day, Bergoglio handed Ortega "the remarks written in his own hand as he recalled them," Magister reported.

On March 13, after the end of the conclave, Ortega asked Pope Francis if he could release the text, and the pope said yes. So on March 26, the photocopy of Bergoglio's manuscript and its transcription in Spanish appeared on the website of *Palabra Nueva,* the magazine of the archdiocese of Havana.

In Bergoglio's remarks one can see some of the key themes in his initial preaching as pope, Magister notes. For example, "spiritual worldliness" is "the worst evil of the Church" and the Church's duty is to "come out from herself" in order to evangelize the "peripheries, not only geographical, but existential."

As on other occasions, Bergoglio here borrows the expression "spiritual worldliness" from the Jesuit Henri de Lubac, one of the greatest theologians of the twentieth century, made a cardinal in his later years by John Paul II. In his book *Meditations on the Church,* de Lubac defines spiritual worldliness as "the greatest danger, the most perfidious temptation, that which always reemerges insidiously when all the others have been overcome, even being fostered by these same victories."

Another significant citation in the notes by Bergoglio is where he points out the dangers to the Church when it ceases to be *"mysterium lunae."*

As Magister explains: "The 'mystery of the moon' is a formula that the Fathers of the Church repeatedly used beginning in the second century to suggest what might be the true nature of the Church and the action that is appropriate to it: like the moon, 'the Church shines not with its own light, but with that of Christ' *(fulget Ecclesia non suo sed Christi lumine),* St. Ambrose says. While for Cyril of Alexandria, 'the Church is enveloped in the divine light of Christ, which is the only light in the kingdom of souls. There is therefore a single light: in this one light nonetheless shines also the Church, which is not however Christ himself.' "

In these final remarks before his election as pope, Bergoglio once again set Christ at the very center of his thought. Here are those "final words" of Cardinal Bergoglio, spoken just four days before his election.

Evangelizing the Peripheries

Reference has been made to evangelization. This is the Church's reason for being. "The sweet and comforting joy of evangelizing" (Paul VI). It is Jesus Christ himself who, from within, impels us.

1. Evangelizing implies apostolic zeal. Evangelizing presupposes in the Church the "parresia" of coming out from itself. The Church is called to come out from itself and to go to the peripheries, not only geographical, but also existential: those of the mystery of sin, of suffering, of injustice, those of ignorance and of the absence of faith, those of thought, those of every form of misery.

2. When the Church does not come out from itself to evangelize it becomes self-referential and gets sick (one thinks of the woman hunched over upon herself in the Gospel). The evils that, in the passing of time, afflict the ecclesiastical institutions have a root in self-referentiality, in a sort of theological narcissism. In Revelation, Jesus says that he is standing at the threshold and calling. Evidently the text refers to the fact that he stands outside the door and knocks to enter. . . . But at times I think that Jesus may be

knocking from the inside, that we may let him out. The self-referential Church presumes to keep Jesus Christ within itself and not let him out.

3. The Church, when it is self-referential, without realizing it thinks that it has its own light; it stops being the *"mysterium lunae"* and gives rise to that evil which is so grave, that of spiritual worldliness (according to De Lubac, the worst evil into which the Church can fall): that of living to give glory to one another. To simplify, there are two images of the Church: the evangelizing Church that goes out from itself; that of the *"Dei Verbum religiose audiens et fidenter proclamans"* [the Church that devoutly listens to and faithfully proclaims the Word of God], or the worldly Church that lives in itself, of itself, for itself. This should illuminate the possible changes and reforms to be realized for the salvation of souls.

4. Thinking of the next Pope: a man who, through the contemplation of Jesus Christ and the adoration of Jesus Christ, may help the Church to go out from itself toward the existential peripheries, that may help it to be the fecund mother who lives "by the sweet and comforting joy of evangelizing."

Rome, March 9, 2013

ACKNOWLEDGMENTS

Every writer depends on others for help, and many have helped me very much in recent weeks, and over the years, as I have written this small volume, and as I have tried to write about the Church and the world over the past twenty-five years.

My son, Christopher Hart-Moynihan, who teaches Spanish at the University of New Mexico, and Maria Pia Carriquiry, daughter of Guzman Carriquiry of Uruguay and Rome, the highest-ranking layperson working in the Vatican and a close friend of Pope Francis, helped me read the homilies in Spanish of Pope Francis while he was the archbishop of Buenos Aires. From their reading came many of the phrases chosen in the final section of this book. Both of them worked very hard, sometimes staying up well after midnight, to complete the task of finding passages which expressed and summed up the thought of the new pope.

During the first days of this new pontificate, when some five thousand journalists filled the Eternal City, and I was asked to comment on what was happening for many television and radio programs, I had the indispensable help of Trey Tomlinson, who went with me, rain or shine, to various studios around the city, and handled for me contacts, schedules, and posting on social media.

Sharlene Lim of the Philippines, who is a student of the

thought of Cardinal Joseph Ratzinger, Pope Emeritus Benedict XVI, came to Rome soon after his resignation. She assisted me throughout the period of preparing this volume, helping to research and organize the material.

William Doino Jr., and my father, William T. Moynihan, helped me with ideas and proofreading.

Gianni Valente and Stefania Falasca contributed time and ideas based on their long friendship with then cardinal Jorge Bergoglio.

Deborah Tomlinson encouraged me from the day the new pope was elected to believe that such a book could be written in the brief time of two weeks and helped throughout the editing and proofreading process. Thanks, Deborah, for your support.

My editor at Random House, Gary Jansen, was also an enormous support during days when the pressure of the deadline for this project seemed heavy. Thank you, Gary.

None of these people are responsible for any of the shortcomings of this work. All of them helped make it possible. Thanks to all of you.

PERMISSIONS

We would like to thank Father Giuseppe Costa and the *Libreria Editrice Vaticana* (the Vatican Press) for granting permission to cite many of Pope Francis's first words: from the balcony of St. Peter's Basilica on March 13; to journalists on March 16; at his first parish mass at St. Anne's Church; at his first Sunday Angelus; at his inaugural Mass on March 19; at his first meeting with fraternal delegates from other Christian churches, and with representatives of non-Chritian religions, on March 20; at his first meeting with diplomats on March 22; and during Holy Week, on Holy Thursday, Good Friday, Holy Saturday, and Easter Sunday; as well as permission to cite from the official Vatican-authorized biography of the new pope; the Vatican's official explanation of the new pope's coat of arms; Father Federico Lombardi's March 14 official Vatican statement on allegations that Cardinal Bergoglio had "collaborated" with the military junta in Argentina during the 1970s; Lombardi's March 23 description of the first meeting of "two popes"; and passages from Pope Emeritus Benedict's historic April 18, 2005, homily, delivered just before he was elected pope.

We would like to thank Sandro Magister, an Italian Vaticanist with *l'Espresso* magazine, for granting permission to use material from his thoughtful writing on the new pope.

We would like to thank Father Claudio Barriga, S.J., Director General Delegate, Apostleship of Prayer, Eucharistic Youth Movement, for permission to cite from an e-mail he wrote about the new pope's first call to the father general of the Jesuit order on March 14, the day after the election.

We would like to thank Catholic News Service for permission to quote from CNS reports on the first days of the new pope, especially the reports by David Agren, "*Porteños* Paint Pope Francis as Kind, Outspoken, Good Administrator," March 17, 2013, and by Carol Glatz, "Pope Makes 'Fantastic Stuffed Calamari' but Often Missed Family Barbecues to Minister," March 24, 2013.

We would like to thank Stefania Falasca and Gianni Valente for permission to cite Stefania's report on her telephone call with the new pope on the evening of March 13, and also her interview with Cardinal Bergoglio, published in *30 Giorni* in 2007.

We would like to thank Catholic News Agency for permission to cite the article "Pope Calls Argentine Kiosk Owner to Cancel Paper Delivery," March 21, 2013.

We would like to thank *The Guardian* newspaper in England for permission to cite material from a March 16, 2013, article by Jonathan Watts and Uki Goni in Buenos Aires, "Pope Francis, the Radical from Flores Who Will 'Reshape' the Catholic Church" and from a March 14, 2013, article by Margaret Hebblethwaite, "The Pope Francis I Know."

We would like to thank Carlos Garde of Rome Reports, for permission to cite text from a March 22, 2013, Rome Reports video.

We would like to thank Andrea Tornielli for permission to quote from an article in *La Stampa/VaticanInsider* on March 25, 2013, "Rosa Margherita, Francis' 'Theologian' Grandmother."

We would like to thank George Demacopoulos, Professor of Theology, Director and Co-Founder, Orthodox Christian Studies Center, Fordham University, for permission to cite from his comments on the new pope's relations with the Orthodox world.

We would like to thank the *Catholic Herald* of London and writer Mary O'Regan for permission to cite passages from O'Regan's thoughtful March 22, 2013, article on the new pope, "A Humble Man Forged in the Dirty War."

We would like to thank Kathryn Jean Lopez, editor-at-large of *National Review Online* and a director of Catholic Voices USA, for granting permission to allow us to publish a few lines from a piece she wrote on the new pope.

We would also like to thank Salon.com for permitting us to cite passages from a March 20 interview by Andrew O'Hehir with actor Viggo Mortensen, titled "Viggo Mortensen: Lay Off the Pope."

We would also like to thank the Canadian Catholic News service and Deborah Gyapong for permission to cite passages from an interview with Archbishop Terrence Prendergast of Ottawa, Canada, on the new pope's Ignatian spirituality, "Jesuit Archbishop Describes the Society of Jesus' Traditions," March 21, 2013.

Mother Teresa: Come Be My Light

The revealing private writings of the Nobel Peace Prize Winner

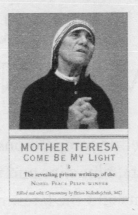

During her lifelong service to the poorest of the poor, Mother Teresa became an icon of compassion. Her selfless commitment to the care of the sick, the dying and thousands of others who no one else was prepared to help, has been recognised and acclaimed throughout the world.

Yet this collection of her writings shows an unexpected picture of the Nobel Peace Prize winner. Her absolute conviction that she was doing God's will is well known but what is a revelation is the discovery that she fulfilled her mission in spite of feeling a chasm of spiritual emptiness within her, which lasted for decades.

This book is a moving chronicle of her spiritual journey, revealing the secrets she shared only with her closest confidants. It illustrates how the experience of an agonizing sense of loss need not hold anyone back from doing something extraordinary with their lives.

£8.99   ISBN 9781846041303

Order direct from www.riderbooks.co.uk

JOIN THE RIDER COMMUNITY

Visit us online for competitions, free books, special offers, film clips and interviews, author events and the latest news about our books and authors:

 www.riderbooks.co.uk

 Rider Books on Facebook

 @Rider_Books

blog riderbooks.tumblr.com

RIDER BOOKS, 20 VAUXHALL BRIDGE ROAD, LONDON SW1V 2SA
E: INFO@RIDERBOOKS.CO.UK